THE
SHAAR
PRESS

THE JUDAICA IMPRINT
FOR THOUGHTFUL PEOPLE

Second

RABBI BEREL WEIN

A
SHAAR
PRESS
PUBLICATION

A collection of musings and observations

Thoughts

Published by **SHAAR PRESS**
Distributed by MESORAH PUBLICATIONS, LTD.
4401 Second Avenue / Brooklyn, New York 11232 / (718) 921-9000

Distributed in Israel by SIFRIATI / A. GITLER BOOKS
10 Hashomer Street / Bnei Brak 51361

Distributed in Europe by J. LEHMANN HEBREW BOOKSELLERS
20 Cambridge Terrace / Gateshead, Tyne and Wear / England NE8 1RP

Distributed in Australia and New Zealand by GOLDS BOOK & GIFT SHOP
36 William Street / Balaclava 3183, Vic., Australia

Distributed in South Africa by KOLLEL BOOKSHOP
22 Muller Street / Yeoville 2198 / Johannesburg, South Africa

ISBN: 1-57819-181-5 Hard Cover
ISBN: 1-57819-182-3 Paperback

Printed in the United States of America by Noble Book Press
Custom bound by Sefercraft, Inc. / 4401 Second Avenue / Brooklyn, N.Y. 11232

Table of Contents

Second Thoughts

Preface

Everyone fancies himself an author, with important things to say. It is therefore extremely human to wish to communicate one's thoughts, opinions, insights, feelings, and even personal revelations to others through the spoken and written word. All of my life I have spoken publicly and privately to people, first as a lawyer and later as a synagogue and community rabbi. I estimate that I spoke and lectured publicly at least 150 times a year for well over three decades in the American rabbinate, and I am continuing apace here in my new life in Jerusalem.

But the spoken word is far different in quality, effect, and influence from the written word. It is only over the last few years that I have begun to write regularly for a general public regarding issues and experiences that are important to me and which could prove interesting and important to others as well. In 1994 I began to publish a monthly newspaper (*The Wein Press*), and a number of years later I undertook to publish weekly essays on the Torah portion of the week, which still appear in a number of Anglo-Jewish newspapers in the United States. When writing for these audiences, I found myself rethinking and refining many of my ideas and positions on current issues, and I was amazed that I had not really thought very deeply about these issues for years. In fact, I realized that I had changed my mind about a great many things, owing to life experience, without admitting it to myself. Thus, the articles and essays that I was writing forced me to come to grips with myself and my beliefs. In truth, this writing experience has touched me, my soul and being, in a way that I never foresaw.

I have collected some of these essays and articles, and reread and rethought them for publication in this current collection. I have edited many of the articles, and I have even rewritten some of them since I am always apparently changing my mind. All of the writings in this book are mine — my opinions, my thoughts, my fears, and my hopes. But although this is a very personal document, I think that it will touch and stimulate you as well, though you certainly are not bound to agree with all of my opinions (even though, as my children can testify, I am always right). The articles have been arranged according to general topics, but in reality many of them are far ranging and not easily classified under any one heading. Then again, human beings and their thoughts and opinions are also not easily fitted under one heading. It is this diversity of mankind that is both the bane and the boon of human civilization. The Rabbis of the Talmud long ago extolled human diversity when they stated that "as no two people are physically alike, so too there are no two people who think exactly alike" on any given issue. So here, for what it is worth, are some of my ideas and thoughts about life-issues that confront us all.

I wish again to thank my friends at Shaar Press and their excellent professional staff for their help in seeing this book through to publication and distribution. My wife, Jackie, who has always encouraged and supported me in my personal and professional life, was especially instrumental in the completion of this book. She has been the greatest of all of the many blessings that the Lord has bestowed upon me in my lifetime. And I am indebted to my many readers who have communicated their opinions, reactions, criticisms, and encouragement to me over the years. Their comments have helped shape my thoughts and have provided the necessary mirror in which I can glimpse myself and assess my ideas.

Though much of the book was written in the United States, its final rewriting and editing was completed in Jerusalem. As such, I feel doubly privileged to see these writings reach you in this book form.

Berel Wein

Jerusalem
MarCheshvan 5758
November 1997

I
CHILDREN AND FAMILY

Children – Never as Planned

The most maddening, frustrating, heart-wrenching experience in human life is raising children. The physical sacrifice, economic cost, and devotion necessary for the task all pale in comparison to the emotional investment involved. For, as all parents can attest, for good and for better, rarely does the project of raising children turn out as planned. The story of the early years of Esav and Jakov, is instructive as to the enterprise of raising children and the sometimes heartbreaking twists and turns of family life. Two brothers, twins, born of the identical genetic stock, raised in the same holy and loving family environment, undoubtedly given equal educational and life opportunities, not only turn out different from one another but become eternal foes. Esav represents the predatory nature of civilization, the survival of the fittest, the exploiter and violent master who views kindness, sensitivity, and humility to others as fatal weaknesses of character. Jakob, in turn, stands for the softer side of civilization. He is scholarly, patient, wonderfully innocent, forbearing, creative, and obedient. Just as these brothers of old warred with each other, so too do their descendants, both physical and spiritual, contest one another to define the nature of society millennia later.

But what of their parents, Isaac and Rebecca? They certainly cannot be happy with Esav and his way of life. Esav's immorality, lust, and violence fly in the face of everything that Abraham and Sarah and Isaac and Rebecca represent. How cruel life must be for Esav's parents when they hear the taunts of the world: "See that murderer, that wanton man, that predator? He is the son of Isaac and Rebecca, the grandson of Abraham and Sarah!" Having succeeded in influencing for the better a large section of their society, Isaac and Rebecca are faced with the horrendous realization that they have produced an ogre in their very own home. In fact are reliving, perhaps to a greater extent, the earlier tragedy of Abraham in greater regard to his son Ishmael. And Jakob himself will also be faced with disappointments and difficulties regarding his own children in a later generation.

The Torah teaches us a humbling lesson. Just as, in all other aspects of life and career, we are subject to inexplicable happenings and unforeseen results, so too in the raising of children and the building of families are we vulnerable to the unexpected, and even undesirable, end product of our sincere and devoted efforts. In all disappointments we are apt to smother ourselves with layers of guilt. A little guilt is always healthy, but we all know instances where perfect parents, such as Isaac and Rebecca, blamelessly produced wicked progeny. How does that happen? Why? It is one of the more inscrutable of G-d's mysteries of human life. The Rabbis acknowledged this when they stated that *bonei tluyei b'mazal* — "[the raising of] children is dependent on good fortune." As parents we are obligated to do all in our power to raise Jacob and not produce Esav. But there are no guarantees, and true success in this task many times cannot be measured for generations. Such is the challenge of life.

Youth

Building the *Mishkan*, the holy tabernacle, in the desert of Sinai was undoubtedly a daunting task. The details of the structure, its appointments, the holy vessels, and the priestly garments were complicated and difficult, both in design and in execution. A great artisan and designer, a person of genius and talent, someone possessed of infinite patience and extraordinary skills, would have to be found in order to fulfill the Divine imperative to "build for Me a tabernacle and I shall dwell in their midst." Such a person was found, the great prototype of all subsequent Jewish builders and artisans — Bezalel, the son of Uri, the grandson of Hur. This talented man was blessed by G–d with extraordinary gifts of creativity and craftsmanship, and the L–rd Himself inspired his work and blessed the labor of his hands. But what makes this choice of Bezalel truly remarkable, almost unbelievable, in fact, is that according to the Talmud (*Sanhedrin* 69b) Bezalel was only 13 years old when he undertook the task of building the *Mishkan!*

It seems that the L–rd Himself, so to speak, was aware that the choice of Bezalel, the 13-year-old boy, would be a perplexing and problematic one. The Talmud (*Berachos* 55a) records that G–d asked Moses his opinion regarding the choice of Bezalel to build the *Mishkan*. Moses responds, "If in Your eyes he is the proper person, then certainly I also agree." G–d nevertheless has Moses consult with the people as Moses did: "If in the eyes of G–d and in the eyes of you, Moses, the choice is a proper one, then we certainly also agree." Yet, in the mere fact that the question is so blatantly posed in the Talmud lies the realization that the choice of the 13-year-old Bezalel is certainly wondrous and strange.

The first Temple in Jerusalem was constructed by King Solomon in the first years of his 40-year reign. Solomon ascended the throne of his father David just before his 13th birthday. Thus, the Jerusalem Temple was also built by a very young person, albeit someone who was already king of Israel. Why this obvious choice of youth over experience, of innocence over hardened maturity?

The building of holy institutions requires a sense of enthusiasm that only youth can provide. When one is young, all things are possible. When one is old, there is not much left that is really possible. Risking capital, opening new ventures, taking outlandish chances is for the young. Conserving capital, retrenching, playing a defensive game is usually the strategy of the old. Building holiness, translating noble and charitable gifts and concepts into physical realities requires daring, energy, unwarranted optimism, and unswerving commitment. These are all the properties of youth. Hence, Bezalel and Solomon became the symbols of all Jewish holy construction for all time. The Jewish people are always described by the prophets as being *naar*, a youth. The Jewish people, the oldest of all peoples, has always remained *naar*, the youngest of all nations. By constantly building ourselves in Torah, we recapture our youthful qualities and are able to embark upon awesome spiritual and physical building projects that other, older societies would not undertake. We are all Bezalel, we are all Solomon. As such, no matter what our chronological age, we are still young and vital, chosen by the G–d of Israel to continue the building of the *Mishkan* in the midst of our society.

My Grandson's Bar Mitzvah

I n the midst of the debacle of the Golden Calf, seemingly defeated and alone, Moses rallies the tribe of Levi, his kinsmen, to his side with the challenge "Whoever is for G–d, let him come now to my side." This very same slogan was raised by an aged Matisyahu at the beginning of his family's campaign against the Syrian Greeks and their Jewish Hellenist supporters. Apparently this battle cry symbolizes the commitment of the hard-core loyalists of Israel to the faith and value system of their ancestors. But how can we be sure that this cry of greatness has not been usurped by pretenders and charlatans, hypocrites and false prophets?

This question has always been valid and troublesome in Jewish life. In today's Jewish society the answer to this question has become absolutely critical to the cause of Jewish survival. Whom shall we follow? Whose voice is the legitimate one in the cacophony of sound that overwhelms us daily? Who is Moses, who is Matisyahu, and who is the *eruv rav*, the homogenized, pluralist destroyers of Israel?

One thing is certain: namely, that this matter must not be settled by current popularity or public opinion. Both Moses and the Hasmoneans could not have mustered a majority vote on their behalf when they shouted, "Who is for G–d, let him come now to my side." For to be "for G–d" is always a lonely and difficult role. Again, it is also usually an unpopular one. It means being non pluralistic and stubborn, anachronistic and subject to the ridicule of the current wisdom. But mostly it means being lonely. And it is this voice which must be heard. The small voice, the quiet voice, the humble voice, the lonely voice, the voice of Isaiah — "a voice that calls in the desert"; the voice that is constant with the Jewish past and tradition, that promises no quick fixes or glittering innovations, that does not tinker with the Torah and introduce new generalities to which it must somehow adjust. The Golden Calf glitters and shines. All of the people dance about it. Joy and singing reign amongst the people of Israel. But today's joy is tomorrow's tragedy, and Moses would rather struggle now and rejoice later than see dancing now and weeping tomorrow. The voice of the halachic, spiritual leaders of Israel is always the one to be heeded, for it alone is the authentic voice of Sinai.

Our grandson, Binyamin HaLevi Teitelbaum, becomes a *bar mitzvah* this Shabbos. There are many hopes and blessings that grandparents have in their hearts for their grandson at a watershed moment in life such as this. But the most important blessing that I feel can be granted to Binyamin is the ability to hear and discern clearly the voice of Moses and Matisyahu amidst all of the other sounds that impress themselves upon a young adolescent in today's society. The task of all Jews is to respond to the question "Who is for G–d?" by rallying and aligning themselves with those true and ancient Torah forces that can alone guarantee purposeful Jewish life and communal survival. Don't be afraid to be different, to be lonely, to be true to your inner self, my beloved Binyamin. There is a lot of aid, counsel, and goodness available to you from others along the way of life. Take advantage of all the wisdom, experience, and help offered to you and don't denigrate any opportunity to learn and benefit from others, especially from your elders and teachers. But always remember that eventually it is all up to you, and you alone. Moses and Matisyahu are waiting for you to come to their side, to be "for G–d," to be a true member of their tribe, the great people and descendants of Levi. Do so and be eternally blessed!

Children as a Blessing

The tradition of Israel has always been to treasure the gift of children. Children were never seen as being mere biological products of human relationships, nor were they seen as chattels to be exploited. The much-maligned caricature of the "Jewish mother" in modern literature bears a kernel of truth, for Jewish parents have always been vitally committed to the welfare of their children, even at abnormally great cost and sacrifice to their personal welfare and comfort. Judaism always viewed children as our vote for the future, our belief in the possibility of a better tomorrow and in the unending eternity of the G–d and people of Israel.

Bearing and raising children is not a logical choice for parents. Children are expensive, noisy, bothersome, spiteful, and often ungrateful and disappointing. And all of this is true of them when they are still little and cute! Older children, grown, married, and now parents themselves, many times are far more hurtful and distressing to their own parents than they were when they were young and living at home. My decades in the rabbinate have provided me with many personal and painful experiences regarding the relationship between parents and children of all ages. Nevertheless, since life is by nature imperfect, the Torah bids us bear, raise, and educate children, and that is seen as one of the highest goals of human — certainly of Jewish — life.

This is the implied message of the Torah laws regarding the status of a woman conceiving and bearing a child. The modern world has adopted a very ambivalent attitude towards children. It loves children, it exploits them in advertising, it exalts them, and it also demeans them. The "populationists" amongst us are always worrying over the increasing numbers of children, and the psychologists are continually warning us not to bruise their fragile psyches. In China, the number of children "allowed" to a married couple is set at one, and that terrible quota is ruthlessly enforced. In the Western world, financial considerations enter into the dropping rate of children born, and, ironically enough, the most severe decline in the birthrate occurs among the most affluent members of society. Apparently, people measure their own comfort vis-a-vis the adjustments and sacrifices that raising children entail, and they vote for their own comfort — for the elusive *now* instead of the unforeseen tomorrow. Children may not always bring comfort to their parents, but Judaism demands that Jews bear, raise, and educate children, no matter how uncertain the *nachas* may be.

The Jewish people are small in number. We have always been so. In this most bloody of human centuries, our numbers have been severely diminished by war, plague, Holocaust, suicidal, irresponsible assimilation and intermarriage. It is unthinkable that Jews should refuse to vote for their future survival and continuity. But by not having children, they stand against faith in our future. Family size and arrangements are personal and private decisions. But the policy of having children and substantial families is Jewish tradition, and in today's Jewish world it is a vital necessity. We are not only a small people; we are also an aging people. Demographic studies have indicated that the Jewish population of America is much older than the average American population. We cannot afford to become old in years or spirit. Our children are our future.

True Hospitality – Did You Ask Your Wife?

One of the basic traits of our father Abraham was his unlimited hospitality towards other human beings. Even pagan Bedouin Arabs were welcomed into his tent, where they were eventually transformed into charitable monotheists. Abraham's hospitality was not only legendary, it also became hereditary. The descendants of his sons Isaac and Ishmael, Jews and Arabs, are committed by their faiths and life-styles to the practice of home and institutional hospitality to the wayfarer, the stranger, the unfortunate, and the underprivileged. In fact, the Talmud raises the practice of such hospitality to a level that surpasses even communion with G–d Himself! As such, there is a vast reservoir of stories, anecdotes, books, and legends regarding this fabled trait of Jewish hospitality throughout the ages and in all climes and circumstances. It seems that everyone must be delighted with the practice of hospitality, and there is no Jew who would not welcome a guest to his Sabbath table or Pesach *Seder* with joy. But, as is true in much of life, the reality of human behavior usually falls short of the ideal so publicly espoused.

The Talmud tells us that the woman of the house is often less than enthusiastic towards guests. This is not a discriminatory remark, nor is it even a critical comment. It is an objective statement regarding the one who really bears the burden of hosting guests in the home. In Biblical and Talmudic times, and even in our day, most, if not all, of the actual work involved in hospitality has been done by the woman of the house. Combined with the constant everyday pressures of housekeeping, child-raising, and food preparation, additional guests, no matter how noble hosting them appears in theory, could easily become distasteful, a source of tension in the house and a resented imposition. The Talmud therefore warns us of this reality, and implicitly cautions us not to ignore the situation.

There are many books currently in vogue extolling the virtues of hospitality, but they are almost exclusively about male hospitality, with the husband inviting countless guests home and the actual work being performed by his long-suffering wife, who was never consulted about the issue. I don't view such a husband as being heroic because of his "hospitable" behavior. The Yiddish expression for such behavior is "that one is a *tzaddik* (a pious person) on someone else's shoulders." Hospitality begins at home. One should be hospitable and considerate first towards one's spouse.

In the description of Abraham's hospitality (Genesis Ch. 18), Abraham is a full partner with Sarah not only in the joys and merit of hospitality, but in its preparation and menial work as well. It is he who "runs to the cattle" to see that the meat for the meal is prepared, while Sarah bakes the bread for the guests. It is Abraham who arranges for seats and water for his guests' needs. He is the consummate host, but not at the cost of overburdening Sarah. True hospitality is a shared family experience, a careful division of labors, as are cleaning and preparation, child-rearing, household chores, and other holy acts. This great trait of hospitality, therefore, leads automatically to strengthening family ties, deepening sensitivity for one another, and creating a home atmosphere that preserves the beauty, warmth, and love which is the heirloom handed down from the tent of Abraham and Sarah to their eternal descendants, the people of Israel.

The Gifted and Self-Motivated

Every teacher loves to teach a class full of self-motivated students. Every employer longs for a staff of workers who are concerned and interested in the success of the company that they are working for. Every parent prays for children who appreciate and understand their particular place and role in the family structure and who therefore don't need constant cajoling, nagging, and reminding about their tasks and chores. But the reality of life is that such individuals are few and far between. The self-motivated student, the unselfish employee, the cheerful, cooperative child are exceptional characters and not the norm of human behavior.

The Talmud teaches us that *kohanim z'rizim heim* — the priestly descendants of Aaron are enthusiastic, self-motivated, even unselfish in the performance of their prescribed duties in the Holy Temple. As such, one might believe that they could be left alone and relied upon thoroughly for the prompt and accurate performance of their Temple duties. However, the Torah, in its unique insight into life and human behavior, takes the opposite view. The comment of the Rabbis on the use of the Hebrew verb *tzav* — command, demand — in the opening verse of the Torah reading *Tzav* is: "*Ein m'zarzin elah l'mzurazin*" — one prods and demands more only from those who are already self-primed and motivated to do better.

This startling view of life is, upon reflection, borne out by the realities of everyday life as we know them. The old adage that "you can bring a horse to water but you cannot force it to drink" speaks volumes about the reality of human behavior. A student who does not wish to study or do well in school will generally not respond well to the efforts of even the greatest educators and psychologists. Slave societies and those that are ruled by totalitarian pressure and terror may initially be productive, fearing the sting of the lash, but eventually they break down, decay, and become hopelessly inefficient and corrupt. The recent demise of the Soviet Union and of the other Communist regimes of Eastern Europe illustrates this historical truth. Encouragement, demands, and challenges only work with those who are already self-challenged. For the others it is mostly a waste of time and effort to push too hard.

A recent study regarding the future of American Jewry, published in the January 1996 issue of *Commentary* magazine and authored by three professors from Hebrew University, Jewish Theological Seminary, and Bar Ilan University, came to a conclusion that has shocked the Jewish Federations establishment in this country. In effect, these scholars now say that the Jewish community should stop wasting its time and money on the intermarried and/or completely unaffiliated and uninterested Jew. That Jew is not interested in "drinking the water" and thus, no matter how attractively a program of Judaism is presented to him, he will not respond to any demands of Jewish "continuity." Instead, the authors recommend that more time, effort, money, and resources be made available to the committed core of American Jews who wish to be more Jewish so that this core can be strengthened, enlarged, challenged, and encouraged. The existence of such a core will automatically provide a new and attractive dynamic to Jewish growth in this country. This is certainly in line with the idea enunciated in the Torah that the committed priests in particular are the ones to be challenged and educated in order to raise them to even greater heights, thereby guaranteeing the continuity of holiness and idealism among the people of Israel.

True Continuity

The basic accomplishment and goal of Jewish life was always defined in terms of generational continuity. The sublime hymn of Jewish praise to the Creator was "from generation to generation will Your acts be praised." To the Jew, the unbroken chain of generations was itself the proof of Torah's eternal truths, as well as the medium through which those truths would be nurtured, preserved, perpetuated and expanded. Thus, Jews were forced to measure their current achievements against a long-term view and could not depend upon their own lifetime accomplishments to be truly meaningful if those accomplishments would not be carried on by the succeeding generation, whether children, friends, or students. Abraham stated this idea when he said to G–d, "L–rd, my G–d, what reward have you given me [seeing that I have no future generation following me], and the master of my house will remain Eliezer of Damascus?" Abraham here does not bemoan his childless state as much as he decries the fact that all of his social, religious, and spiritual accomplishments will die with him in the absence of heirs committed to his value system and life-style. The first Jew already thought in terms of eternal generational continuity as the sole vindication of his lonely path of life in a dark, hostile, and pagan world.

But fathering/mothering children by itself does not guarantee generational continuity. At an advanced age, Abraham is blessed with a son, Ishmael, and 13 years later with a second son, Isaac. In spite of all the efforts of Abraham, Ishmael is unwilling to follow in his footsteps. He, unfortunately justifiably, acquires a terrible reputation as a man of violence and crime, "his hand against all, and everyone's hand against him." How disappointed Abraham must have been at this turn of events! Abraham, the man of peace, justice, kindness, and hospitality, finds his life's accomplishments apparently negated by his own son. What scorn and derision must have been heaped upon him by his society, which, like all later societies, was quick to criticize and slow to sympathize. Yet Abraham remembers G–d's promise, that somehow through Isaac, he will yet find continuity, vindication, and eternity. Therefore, Abraham spares no effort or cost to find for Isaac the proper mate and to ease Isaac's path in becoming his successor in the world. For without Isaac, Abraham's lifelong struggle for G–d and man is doomed to defeat.

Children are a very chancy project. In spite of all material and spiritual efforts, tuition and camps, instructions and guidance, all children must eventually go their own way, independent of their parents' wishes, hopes, and prayers. There are no guarantees that the path they choose will preserve the parents' ideals and Jewish way of life in the next generation. Our times — in fact, all the times of Jewish history — are replete with incidents of pious parents with impious descendants. The pain of the parents in such cases is infinite and immeasurable. Yet the nature of life makes such situations unavoidable. Rather than despair, Abraham redoubles his efforts to guarantee his continuity through Isaac and eventually prevails.

Our generation, with its rampant intermarriage rates on one hand and the strengthening of the core of Torah in Jewish life on the other hand, stands in the shoes of our father Abraham. May we also find triumph and solace in the generation of Isaacs that will follow us.

The Multifaceted Person

Phinehas, as described in the Torah and even later in the books of Joshua and Judges, appears to be a most enigmatic character. He is described as a *kanaai* — a zealot who rises to a difficult situation and takes immediate and violent action to rectify a perceived wrong. He is also described as a *kohen* — a priest, a grandson of Aaron, one "who loves peace, pursues peace, loves people, and attempts to bring them closer to Torah." He is also the *kohen mashuach milchamah* — the priest who accompanied the Jewish army when it entered battle, attempting thereby to bring succor and spiritual inspiration to soldiers engaged in the brutality of war. So which of the above roles is representative of the real Phinehas? Is he the zealot or the man of peace and warmth? Is he the "chaplain" who attends to the needs of his soldier wards in the trenches of battle, or is he the High Priest wearing his golden vestments in the Temple in Jerusalem? Who is the essential Phinehas?

The simple answer to this question is that Phinehas is a composite of all the above roles. Human beings are very hard to categorize. All of us are different people at different times, under varying circumstances. We are all zealots when the occasion for zealotry truly arises. We are all peaceful and compassionate when that response is appropriate to the situation. We see ourselves as the comforter of endangered fighters and the representatives of G–d and Israel in holy service. But the challenge in all of these scenarios is to be the right Phinehas, at the right time, under the right circumstances. Being a zealot while representing G–d and Israel in the Temple, a compassionate and sensitive person in the midst of the struggle of battle, a holy and other-worldly priest when action and decisive behavior are required, all are wrong responses and definitely not productive for Jewish society.

My great teacher, Rabbi Mendel Kaplan, would repeatedly tell us that every student in the yeshivah must also be a sophisticated person in worldly matters. He would always ruefully add, however, that when the simplicity and innocence of a yeshivah student is required, the cynical and sophisticated man of the world often takes over, and when sophistication and worldliness are the proper responses to the situation, suddenly the yeshivah student arrives. The greatness of Phinehas lay not only in his ability to be so many people at once, but to display each aspect of his personality at the right time and in the right situation. That is truly a mark of greatness and adds to the heroic luster of Phinehas.

My beloved grandson, Dovid Shmaya HaLevi Teitelbaum, read the Torah portion of Pinchas as he celebrated his *bar mitzvah*. Even though the future remains shrouded in mystery for all humans, it is certainly safe to assume that he will face many challenges and differing situations in his future. His years of Torah study, the security and serenity of his family environment, and his own multiple talents and gracious personality will all stand him in good stead in the years to come. But Dovid, like all of us, will have to marshal all his talents and efforts and the various facets of his personality to deal with life's challenges. I hope that when the times call for leadership and boldness, Dovid will emulate the original Phinehas in his own life.

II
LIFE'S
CYCLES

Retirement

One of the more difficult decisions in life is when, or even if, one should retire from his work of decades. No one ever enjoys being told that his services are no longer required, and, speaking from personal experience, I doubt if there are many people who relish the task of having to make this announcement to someone else. But life and society constantly require renewal, and therefore the old and established always must make room for the new and the future. The wise person heeds the wisdom of Solomon, who said that "there is a time for everything," and gracefully leaves at the right time. We are all witness to politicians, performers, and other public figures who stay on too long. They evoke within us feelings of annoyance and derision, albeit mixed with understanding pity. It has become a cliche of our time that one should leave while he is still "at the top of his game." But the problem in life is that one may feel that he is at the top of his game when most others feel that the game is already over. We are therefore often confused and emotionally hurt when confronted by arbitrary, mandatory retirement ages, and feel that the guidelines of youth are unnecessarily impersonal and rigid. We feel discarded and rejected; and retirement for many, therefore, is not a "golden" period but rather a time of depression and emotional trauma. With the blessed increase in our life expectancy comes the downside of retirement.

The Torah delineates for us the years of labor of the Levites in the *Mishkan* — the Tabernacle of Israel built in the Sinai desert which remained for centuries the focal point of Jewish public worship of G–d. We are told that the Levites worked in the Tabernacle for 20 years, from the age of 30 until the age of 50. However, the Talmud tells us that the mandatory retirement age of 50 was only enforced in the *Mishkan*, where heavy labor such as carrying and transporting the frame and artifacts of the *Mishkan* was required, but which no longer applied once the great Temple was built in Jerusalem. In that sanctuary, there was no mandatory retirement age, either for priests (*kohanim*) or Levites. The Talmud tells us that the time of retirement for these servants of G–d and Israel in the Temple was dependent not on age but on continuing physical and mental prowess. This appears to be a much fairer scale than the arbitrary age barrier of 50 or 65, or any other age. Yet we are still left with the problem of who is to pass judgment on the physical and mental ability of the aging person. And, no matter how objective the standards for such judgment appear to be, such decisions are ultimately personal and subjective.

The Talmud teaches us that Torah personalities, scholars of Israel, age gracefully. They are never retired from public service, for the older they become, "the more settled and balanced their minds and personalities become." Those, however, who are far removed from Torah in their earlier years and who maintain their distance from their heritage will find the retirement years frightening and disjointed. I have known many people in my years in the rabbinate who made a new spiritual life for themselves in their retirement years. They joined Torah study classes, participated daily in synagogue life and prayer, and gave the gift of inner religious growth and caring to themselves and to others. The retired *kohanim* and Levites of ancient Israel became the teachers and mentors of the younger generation, not only in terms of formal Torah education, but as role models. They taught the benefits of a life well spent and of goals achieved, communally and spiritually. There is no higher calling than this.

The Silent Response

There is no right time for tragedy and sadness. The Angel of Death is hardly ever a welcome visitor, yet there are times when his appearance is particularly horrifying and heart breaking. The prophet Jeremiah declares that sometimes "death jumps through our window" instead of entering genteelly through the front door. Recent terrorist attacks in Israel which have killed and maimed scores of innocents in a sudden furious moment of carnage bring the prophet's metaphor to mind. But there are other, less dramatic forms of this tragic phenomenon that occur with some regularity in "normal" human life — automobile accidents, the death of the young, sudden death in the midst of active life. Without warning or preparation, death hideously "jumps through our window." What is the reaction of a good and normal person in such circumstances of personal desolation? How can life go on after such a sudden and seemingly capricious blow?

The Torah gives an example of how to deal with such a tragic event. At a moment of supreme joy and accomplishment in the lives of both Moses and Aaron, inexplicable and unforeseen tragedy strikes. As the two oldest sons of Aaron, Nadab and Abihu, are installed as priests in the service of the *Mishkan* —

the Tabernacle of G–d — they are struck down by heaven-sent fire which consumes their lives and ends their careers before they have begun. Moses, Aaron, the grief-stricken mother of the victims, and the entire congregation of Israel are trauma-tized. The Torah tells us that the response of the great holy man of Israel, Aaron the High Priest, is one of passive silence. "*Vayidom Aharon,* and Aaron was silent" — that is his re-sponse to the unfathomable tragedy. Shaken by his loss, Aaron nevertheless refuses to debate the matter with his Creator. In-stinctively realizing that he will never really understand the inscrutable wisdom and, yes, compassion of the good Creator, Aaron remains silent. The legendary Job, finding himself in similar circumstances, takes a different approach. He rails against his fate, declares his complete innocence and blame-lessness, and debates the seeming injustice of the event with man and G–d. But after all of the words and poetry, the pos-turing and accusations, the passion and pathos of Job's statements, he eventually must also accept Aaron's path of si-lence and acceptance as being the only possible way to deal with tragedy and move on, as best one can.

One of the great heroic chapters in Jewish history has been written in our time by the survivors of the Holocaust. Most of them went on to build new and productive lives for themselves after their release from the horrors of Hitler and Stalin. Most of them never spoke about their experiences, even though the memories never left any one of them for an instant during their entire lives. Most children of Holocaust survivors testify that their parents never spoke to them about "it." Only now, over 50 years later, are some of the survivors willing to talk, and now only because they are afraid that the Holocaust itself will be de-nied, or even worse, forgotten, if they continue to remain silent. Yet the truth is that silence was the most fitting initial response to that awful stain on humanity's conscience. G–d is not heard in noise or fire or wind but in the almost silent, still voice of his-tory. Aaron's response — *vayidom* — "and he was silent," somehow remains the typical — and proper — Jewish response to the tragedy that "jumps through our window."

Patience

The sad story of the bitter tragedy of the Jews in the desert and the Golden Calf has many relevant and important messages for our times. The basic catalyst for the Golden Calf incident was the impatience of the Jewish people. The Torah itself describes the scene: "And the people saw that Moshe was delayed in returning to them from the mountain of Sinai ..." This delay caused a feeling of frustration, fear, and severe impatience to sweep through the encampment of the Jewish people. "Where is he? What happened to him? What will happen to us now that he is not here?" These were the questions that troubled Israel. And these feelings of malaise and doubt eventually led to the creation of the Golden Calf.

Paganism not only supplied attractive and simplistic answers to human problems, it also supplied them quickly. The Greek oracles of old never kept their clients waiting or in doubt. Reward and punishment from the pantheon of the pagan gods were always instantaneous and unambiguous. Not so the relationship of the G–d of Israel with the human race. To have any sort of spiritual relationship with our Creator requires time, effort, and above all else, patience. G–d, Who is beyond time, waits even to the one-thousandth generation to balance the books. We, whose life span is compressed and short, cannot even judge correctly the current events that surround us. It is our impatience that drives us to commit folly and error. We are always driven to "do something" when perhaps the wisest course is to wait and do nothing. Moshe eventually returns to the camp from the mountain, but by then Israel has "done something" that Moshe will have to undo and that the Jewish people will have to pay for over many generations.

One of the negative hallmarks of our generation is impatience. We are impatient with our spouses and our marriages, with our children and their problems and weaknesses, with our schools and educational systems, with our governments, with our fellow drivers on the road, and above all else, with ourselves. We are therefore driven to "do something," to build Golden Calf situations for ourselves, to follow every new whim and fashion, no matter how patently erroneous and foolish it is, and we pay an enormous price for our impatience. My experience as a lawyer taught me that a deal entered into because of impatience is always a bad deal, whether it is in business or real estate, or part of a "peace process." G–d's wisdom can only be glimpsed by mortal man over a span of time, which is why knowledge and appreciation of history and tradition are so important for the achievement of stability and serenity in life. I have always ruefully maintained that a school's success with a student lies in the following formula: 90% patience, 10% good fortune. That statement may be too facetious, but the patience requirement is certainly true. And it takes a lot of patience to learn how to be patient. The lesson of the Golden Calf is one we must always remember.

Grief and Solace

Our mother Sarah, the faithful wife and life companion of Abraham, dies suddenly and alone. Abraham comes to Hebron to eulogize and bury her. The Torah notes that he came "to weep for her." Rabbi Samson Raphael Hirsch, in his commentary on the Torah, indicates that the Hebrew word used in the Biblical text for "weeping" — *livkosah* — according to our Masoretic text tradition contains a small *kaf.* He explains this anomaly by stating that Abraham did not express his full grief at the death of his beloved Sarah in a public manner, but rather contained it within his psyche and soul. The infinite feeling of bereavement that he felt at Sarah's death was so personal that it could never find public expression. Though his tears were no longer visible, though Sarah had lived a long and nobly productive life, Abraham never stopped weeping inwardly for the loss of his life's companion and soulmate. The Rabbis of the Talmud articulated this truth when they stated, *"Ein ishah meisah ela l'baalah* — A wife's death is felt in its fullness only by her husband." The end of Sarah, even though it preceded Abraham's death by many decades, also marked an end for Abraham. Such is life and the bittersweet cup that it extends to all of us to drink from.

The Torah also records for us the joyous event of the marriage of Isaac and Rebecca. Just as death marks the final chapter of life, so does marriage mark the beginning of the most productive and important period of human existence. The finding of one's partner and the physical and spiritual bond that is created by marriage serves to erase past hurts and to ease previous disappointments and tragedies. The Torah tells us, *"Vayevi'eha ha'ohelah Sarah imo* — Isaac brought her into the tent of his mother Sarah." Rashi explains that all of the wondrous aspects of Sarah's home — in fact those hallmarks of the traditional Jewish home throughout the ages — that Isaac sorely missed after the death of his mother were now fully restored by the presence of his wife. The Torah sums up the matter succinctly: *"Vaye'ehaveha vayinacheim Yitzchok acharei imo* — And he [Isaac] loved her [Rebecca], and Isaac thereby found solace after the loss of his mother."

Solace is found in the love of another human being. It is found in the loyalty, fidelity, responsibility, and spirituality that a successful marriage demands. In the creation of new life, in the holiness of creating a shelter for the next generation, in the determined transmission of ancient traditions and values, one may find compensation for past losses and relief from traumatic difficulties. But again, it is in the nature of life that it is Isaac, the son, who finds consolation for the loss of his mother. The Torah nowhere mentions that Abraham is ever truly consoled by a specific event after the death of Sarah.

The realistic, normal, healthy view of life that the Torah portrays is itself a source of comfort and faith for us. The Torah is very wary of extremes of emotion and behavior. Both joy and grief have their times and their limits. The tradition and *halachah* of Israel allows us to deal with life's cycle in a healthy, productive, and even serene fashion. In this respect we may truly say that *"maaseh avos siman l'banim* — the example of our fathers is the guide for the children."

Death

In the discussion of the creation of life on this planet, which is the centerpiece of the first portion of the Torah, the Midrash informs us, based on the language and terms used here, that while life is "good," death is somehow "very good." This startling statement begs explanation. When and how does death become "very good"? And even if there are individual circumstances — enormous pain, fear of torture, idealistic martyrdom — that can attempt to justify the "goodness" of death, the words of the Midrash are purposely general and speak about the universal cycle of life and death rather than unique, individual circumstances. And does it not appear from the Torah itself that death was a punishment, a curse, placed upon Adam and Eve and their descendants, because of their sinful behavior? If this is the case, where is there room for the interpretation of "very good" in the matter of death?

This problem has been the subject of much commentary and philosophy over the ages. We are transfixed by death and have an unquenchable curiosity about it. People have always been willing to turn out to see a hanging. There are always many applications to prison authorities for permission to witness executions, even in the most civilized of societies. Probably many more people are squeamish about witnessing birth than about witnessing death. All of this is because death grips us intently during our lifetime. It is never far from us, and its unseen but deeply felt presence exerts enormous influence over our behavior. For death forces upon us the ultimate question: "What is life?"

And to that question there are then only two possible answers: either life is nothing and what we do in the world matters not one whit; or life is everything, and because of that belief, everything that humans do has great and lasting cosmic effect. It is the presence of death that forces humans to come to grips with the meaning of life. The Torah tells us that if Adam had eaten from the fruit of the tree of life, humans would have "lived forever." The Torah, by its tone, indicates that this would not be a happy or productive state of being for mankind. It is death that gives life urgency, direction, meaning, and a true sense of human greatness and possibility. Without the awareness of death, perhaps man would never search for his true inner self, his immortal soul, his connection with creation and the Creator.

The Midrash points out that humans still retain the ability to "live forever" and that the "tree of life" therefore still resides in the midst of our earthly garden of physical life. However, these terms have been redefined to fit our mortal state of being. Every act, word, attitude, and behavior pattern of our physical, fleeting life will indeed, in a spiritual sense, "live forever," either in nobility or in infamy. That realization makes life sacred and even death somehow "very good." For it represents the triumph of the "tree of life" — of holy values, tried and tested traditions, the truth of the Creator and His Torah — in the midst of our garden of worldly life. In spite of all advances in technology and civilization, humans are still bedeviled by the original spiritual angst that faced Adam and Eve. Therefore, our task, just as theirs, is to make our lives "very good" in the eyes of G–d and man.

Human Frailties

The human capacity for greatness is unlimited. So, apparently, is the human capacity for failing and weakness. When we think of "religion," we almost invariably think of the capacity for greatness, and we do not often dwell on the weaknesses that are inherent in our mortal condition. "Religion" usually ignores man's problems and shortcomings, and instead insists on emphasizing his potentially holy nature. Perhaps this is as it should be if we are interested in furthering good in the world, but any observer who is experienced in the vagaries of human affairs knows that emphasizing man's holy nature while ignoring his ever-present failures, vices and disappointments is unrealistic in the extreme. The attitude of Judaism and especially the *halachah* (the laws of behavior) of Judaism is to confront and deal with human weaknesses directly and honestly. The realism and honesty of Jewish thought and law regarding the true nature of man and the real problems of life is the source of its eternal strength. Life means facing problems and defects, not hiding from them.

Thus, we read in the Torah of the reality that soldiers sometimes take women as captives and "marry" them. The Torah prescribes a course of behavior and a strict set of protective measures to prevent the abuse of the captive woman. Such rules, with which the Jewish soldier is familiar, should perhaps give that soldier pause before "marrying" the woman. Yet the

Torah recognizes that this scenario usually involves an instant of passion, not planned behavior, and thus the Torah deals with the "after" of the situation and attempts to construct a future for the woman and her soldier husband. In addition, there is the realization that even under ideal circumstances, marriages sometimes just don't work. The Torah and the Jewish life-style has always been very family oriented and anti-easy-divorce. Yet the Torah expresses the realization that there are situations that necessitate divorce. Again, the Torah legislates the procedure and attitude to be followed when this sad but sometimes necessary situation emerges in Jewish life.

Also described in the Torah reading is the child that is every parent's dreaded nightmare — the "one I can't do anything with." Even though the Talmud views this portion of the Torah as being purely theoretical, in the hope that the child's punishment will never be put into practice in Jewish life, the moral of the story of the incorrigible child is clear: Sometimes one must protect one's own life, family, and community from the ravages of an uncontrollable and malevolent person, even if that person is one's own child or brother. A proactive response is necessary to save everyone, even the child himself, from the terrible consequences of his decidedly antisocial behavior. All babies are adorable and promising. But some of them develop into cruel, sadistic people. The Torah wants us to recognize that reality of human life.

The Torah also discusses the problem of inheritances. There is probably no other issue that destroys families as often as the inheritance of wealth. Children somehow feel cheated, and sibling rivalry often becomes family war when a parent's inheritance is involved. The Torah addresses this problem as well with a set of laws. Jewish law teaches that if someone wills money to a trustee to "do with it the best deed he can," the rule is that the "best deed he can" is to distribute it to the deceased's children in accordance with the laws of the Torah. The willingness to abide by the rules of Torah, and to know in advance that those are the rules that will be followed, will go a long way to preserve family unity in the face of the temptation to fight for inheritance money.

These examples of life's difficulties and the Torah discipline necessary to help humans deal with these difficult situations are the backbone of Torah values and attitudes generally.

Goodbye and Hello

On July 28, 1997, my wife, my father, and I departed from our home in Monsey, New York, to take up permanent residence in Jerusalem. I have been working on the realization of this move for at least 30 years, and therefore, this move is literally a dream fulfilled. Over the past five years, my wife and I have been able to spend a substantial portion of each year in Jerusalem, and this will undoubtedly aid in our adjustment to our new situation.

But, truth be told, until July 28 Monsey was always our real home. Even when we were in Jerusalem for long periods of time, we were always going "home" to Monsey. There, Shaarei Torah was my school/yeshivah, and Congregation Bais Torah was my synagogue. We had lived in our comfortable home on Hilltop Place for 25 years. We knew every nook and cranny of that house, we heard every familiar sound it made in the stillness of night, and it housed the accumulations, both tangible and intangible, of over four decades of family life. We had wonderful neighbors, and every one of our acquaintances, including the sanitation men, the mailperson (she is a woman), the gardener, and the regular money collectors, had become our friends, part of our lives. And now, all of this has changed, for we are no longer going "home" to Monsey after the summer. No more Shaarei Torah, no more Bais Torah, no more Hilltop Place, no more Monsey. Yes, we'll visit and we'll see all of our Monsey students, congregants, and friends regularly here in Israel or on our family visits to the United States, but it will be different. For we have moved away, and our "home" is now Ben Maimon Boulevard in Jerusalem, and the Monsey chapter of our lives is closed.

If I had known in advance how gut wrenching, sad, emotionally draining, and tear laden, saying goodbye would be, I would perhaps have been less insistent on uprooting my father and my wife and moving to Jerusalem now. But the wonderful part about moving, just as in married life, is that no one can anticipate the difficulties and emotions involved. It is only when one passes through the experience that the true reality of the situation and the depths of the emotions that it creates are revealed. And thus, even though a large piece of my heart and mind still resides in Monsey, I am now irrevocably a Jerusalemite. I have passed through the crucible of Israeli bureaucracy (not too bad an experience, really — the Department of Motor Vehicles is the same the world over!), and I speak in a heavily accented American/Chicago dialectal Hebrew. I have made friends with some essential people here in this country — the secretary at the medical clinic in which I am enrolled, the lady at the window of my local post office who handles my mail and bill payments, the assistant manager at the bank (this is the single most important contact, since no one here, even the bankers, can figure out how to make a normal, simple transaction in a reasonable amount of time), and a barber who is not interested in discussing his or my personal life while cutting what is left of my hair. But still, everything is new, everything is strange, and some things are downright intimidating and scary. What a great adventure life in Jerusalem is going to be!

Jerusalem's welcome to her children is a slow and undemonstrative one. Jerusalem does not stun you or overwhelm you. It grows upon you, slowly, day by day, person by person, experience by experience. The city itself is beautiful, its stone buildings shimmering in the golden sun, its roadways lined with flowers and greens, its public buildings understated and comforting. The city is very old and gives a feeling of antiquity still alive. The city is also very new, with buildings under construction everywhere, traffic jams that remind me of driving across Manhattan at rush hour, and enormous shopping malls.

But mainly, the city is indefinable in concrete, physical terms alone. Jerusalem is basically a time-line of history, and living here makes one acutely aware that G–d intended us all to be participants in the drama of civilization and not merely observers. It is this sense of history and destiny that slowly grows upon the newcomer. One eventually realizes that living in Jerusalem is not restricted to the fulfillment of a personal dream, but rather is part of a much larger vision and process. Everyone has a part to play in the realization of that great prophetic vision, and in Jerusalem one appreciates that obligation more clearly and decisively, perhaps, than anywhere else.

Having an idealized picture of Jerusalem or of Israel, or of the Jewish people in general, is dangerous, for it invariably sets one up for major disappointment and disillusionment when the harsh reality of daily life here confronts him. On the whole, life here is wonderful, but there are moments and moments, people and people, life-styles and life-styles. It is therefore important to remember the wise words of a Jerusalemite who came here from Poland in 1793. Rabbi Abraham HaCohen of Kalisk wrote: "Behold, one arrives here with his Talmudic and Torah knowledge in hand, with his habits and customs intact, and finds it difficult to adjust to the new environment. He finds no rest, his mind depresses him; where is the Torah life, the observance of commandments, the serenity and peace of the Holy Land? And suddenly, in his moment of deepest depression, the L–rd shows grace unto him, and calm and serenity begin to descend upon him. This event of redemption knows no time frame, and one can never predict when it will arrive. It will depend upon the nature, behavior, and spiritual circumstances of each individual and the status of the person's soul. But eventually the moment will come. Therefore, he who wishes to come to this country should analyze his personal temperament and stamina, and decide if he will be able to stand up to all of the difficulties involved. If he is truly devoted and his character traits are correct, then may he come in all security and surely find rest and serenity for his soul here." Good advice and a realistic assessment of the Holy Land for all times.

III
TIMES AND THOUGHTS

Yom Kippur

Yom Kippur provides Jews with two of the most valuable gifts that a human being can receive. The first is the ability to find a moment of privacy, of serenity, of self, of introspection. Even though modern life is very busy and noisy, it is also basically lonely, with much sadness and depression. Because of this, people find it difficult to be alone with themselves. But without that gift of privacy and introspection, we would never have the ability to think of ourselves in a spiritual, cosmic, and eternal sense. We are always bidden to be our own main judges, for we alone are aware of our true selves and inner status. Who am I? Where am I in life's journey? Who would I like to be? How do I wish to be remembered? What can I do about myself and those I love? What does it mean to be a Jew? Why should I wish to remain Jewish? Why is it worth it to struggle to remain Jewish? What is death? Am I immortal, and what does that mean? These are things that we rarely think about. They are troubling questions, but they are the most necessary questions that we can ever ask. And the holy day of Yom Kippur — no work, no food, no telephones, no media, no money, no distractions — with its privacy and meditation, fasting and praying, thinking and committing, provides us with the background and opportunity to deal with these questions, and to deal with our longing for eternity.

The second gift of Yom Kippur is the opportunity for a second (or third or fourth) chance in life. Even superficial repentance has the power to arrest evil. True, gut-wrenching, sincere, tearful repentance can even *reverse* the scars of evil within us. It is enormously difficult to admit, "I was wrong. I am sorry." But if there is anything that is representative of Yom Kippur, it is this quality of regret, apology, repentance, and continual renewal. Yom Kippur affords us an opportunity for a clean (or at least cleaner) slate upon which to write our future. It does not allow us to wallow in self-pity, in self-condemnation (which is also somehow neurotically satisfying), or in hopelessness. Yom Kippur is tomorrow and all of our tomorrows. It assesses and balances our past; but more importantly, it charts and sets our future. What a day of opportunity and hope!

Central to the day of Yom Kippur is the community of the people of Israel. Repentance, forgiveness, and spiritual renewal are not only individual priorities on that day, they are national communal goals of the Jewish people as a whole. There are those who demand that the Jewish community accept them on their own terms, with their present agendas. In effect, they are lobbying for an exclusively private Yom Kippur, one that does not force them to confront Sinai and tradition. But all of Jewish history has taught us that it is the *public* Yom Kippur, the linkage of all the generations of Israel — a linkage possible only through the commitment to the Torah and its precepts — that guarantees both individual and national survival, continuity and holiness. The commandment to be a holy people, to be a holy community, is always expressed in the Torah in the plural form of "you." Because of this emphasis on the general society and not only on the individual person, the true forgiveness and redirection of purpose which is inherent in Yom Kippur demands the alignment of the individual with the traditions and holy goals of Sinai and tradition, no matter his personal wants, needs, and predilections. May we all be renewed on this holy day for life and purpose, serenity, and the successful pursuit of eternity.

Curiosity, Inquiry, and Freedom

Slavery rarely allows time for questioning and philosophizing. The sad status of persecution and the absence of control over one's life leaves little room for contemplation of the meaning of life and the purpose of existence. The slave wishes only to be free of the lash and the chain. Thus, a phenomenon exists in human history, one which has been noticed and discussed by many scholars: As long as the bonds of slavery are held very tightly, there is little or no intellectual ferment and a drive for spiritual freedom or intellectual analysis amongst the oppressed. However, once the bonds are loosened, apparently even slightly, all of the resentments, questions, rebelliousness, and frustration contained within the slave society erupts, many times with violent and destructive force.

The Torah itself points to this phenomenon. In describing the obligations of the Passover service at the time of the Jewish people's exodus from Egypt, it raises for the first time the overriding issue of doubt and faith, of the meaning of being Jewish, of life itself: "And when your children shall ask you, What meaning does this service [of Passover] have for us? You shall answer them..." Now, when the shackles of slavery have been broken and the long-sought-after freedom has been achieved, the Torah tells us that you may be certain that "your children shall

ask you." For freedom creates the climate of inquiry and questioning, of probing and discovering and deciding. A hallmark of
human freedom is that it spawns differences of opinions, encouraging it and providing the intellectual and spiritual
parameters that allows the debate to be productive, ennobling,
and eternal.

For reasons that are not understandable to me, there are
many parents who stifle their children's curiosity. Questions are
not answered or sometimes even allowed. In withholding from
their children the freedom of questioning, searching, even
doubting, parents make a disastrous mistake that will affect
their family negatively, sometimes for generations. Especially in
our generation, when communication potential is enormous
and the world is very small, children's questions, doubts, fears,
and searchings are to be addressed and not ignored. The Torah
assures us that there will come a day "when your children shall
ask you," and therefore, parents had better be prepared for that
moment. Intellectual ferment is a natural by-product of freedom. The Torah ordains, and all of life confirms, this pattern of
human behavior. It would be foolish for parents, educators, and
communal leaders to ignore this clear message of the Torah and
of Jewish history.

The Passover service is built upon the principle of question-
and-answer, of intellectual give-and-take. But this attitude and
exercise of freedom should not be seen as being restricted to
the Passover service itself. It is sad beyond words to train children to ask the "four questions" at the Passover *Seder* and then
deny them that right to question during the rest of the year.
Questioning develops answers, supports faith, encourages
thoughtful analysis, and is part of Jewish tradition. Telling children, students, or in fact anyone, that they do not have the right
to question but must only accept and obey is counter productive. Only in matters of Torah law and the principles of faith
must a Jew be accepting without question. What an important
lesson for all of us to contemplate in our lives and families.

The Sabbath

The commandment and concept of the Sabbath is central to all meaningful Jewish life. The erosion of Sabbath observance, or even Sabbath commemoration, among the masses of Israel is the single most heartbreaking phenomenon of modern Jewish life. For without the Sabbath, full assimilation and intermarriage become almost inevitable. There is no reliable safeguard of Jewish communal life other than the Sabbath. Not nationhood, not grand structures or tabernacles, not even shared experience and common fate will guarantee Jewish survival. But the commemoration and observance of the Sabbath will guarantee that survival. A famous Jewish writer and *maskil* ("enlightened" person) of the 19th century, not particularly known for his pro-Torah views, nevertheless remarked ruefully: "More than the Jews have kept the Sabbath, the Sabbath has kept the Jews." The general wave of spiritual amnesia that has overwhelmed most of Jewry and its secular leadership today has erased this recognition from the conscious mind of the Jewish people. But forgotten or ignored realities are still realities, and the reality of Jewish existence is that only through the Sabbath will we be able to find our way back to our inner spiritual home.

In light of this, it becomes perfectly clear why the Torah, in recounting the story and many details of the building of the *Mishkan*, blends into that narrative the strict demand for the observance and commemoration of the Sabbath. In fact, the Oral Law designates the actual labors performed in the building of the *Mishkan* as the halachic underpinning of the Sabbath day itself, determining and defining for us the concept of "work" that is prohibited on that day. The Torah teaches us that even a *Mishkan*, a holy public sanctuary built through the sacrifice and efforts of all the Jewish people, will be unable to fulfill its proper role — in fact, unable to survive itself — without the commemoration and observance of the holy Sabbath day within the community of Israel. All of the great Temples and sanctuaries of Israel have been destroyed at one time or another in the course of the long Jewish story. Yet the people survived and somehow even thrived under the worst of circumstances. That was because the buildings may have been destroyed, but not the Sabbath. What a lesson! What a warning!

Building a *Mishkan* is a very precarious venture. Building projects, whether personal or communal, take on a life and dimension all their own. They run away with our money, our time, often the very spirit of the owner or builder. In most instances, in spite of our strongest efforts, the completed building project leaves us somehow unfulfilled and a bit frustrated. We should have eliminated this post or made that closet larger or made more skylights or fewer skylights or moved the window or ... The craftsmen, no matter how devoted or expert they may be, are always imperfect, for such is the nature of humans. Bezalel's *Mishkan* was apparently the exception to all of these rules. Nevertheless, it also did not last. Most of it was later absorbed into Solomon's Temple, which was no longer a "perfect" building, as the *Mishkan* had been, for the Temple was built by human craftsmen without Divine intervention (except for the *shamir* of the stonemasons).

But the Sabbath, in all of its uniqueness, remains eternal, warming and illuminating each and every generation of Jews through its holy fire and spiritual light. It is the Sabbath that is the hero of the story of the construction of the *Mishkan*. It is the Sabbath that is the hero of all Jewish life and the secret of the survival of Israel. Let us therefore welcome the Sabbath Queen and give thanks for this great gift of G–d's every day of our lives.

The Chanukah Stamp

The United States Postal Service, for the first time in its history, issued a "Chanukah stamp" for the holiday season of 1996. This completes the dereligiousization (is there such a word?) of the Chanukah holiday in the eyes of American society. A decade ago, in a landmark decision, the United States Supreme Court decided, incredibly, that the Chanukah "menorah" was not a religious symbol but only a social symbol, such as the Christmas tree. Hence, there was no violation of the constitutional principle decreeing the separation of Church and State, and the Chanukah "menorah" could be displayed on public or government property without violating the intent of our founding fathers. The Chanukah postage stamp therefore proudly takes its place with the annual Christmas stamp as a social symbol of the morality and diversity of the United States.

Like most developments in public life, this Chanukah stamp issuance cuts two ways. The positive side of the matter is the confirmation of how deeply the Jewish community has rooted itself — and more importantly, how widely it has been accepted — in American life, culture, and society. It is inconceivable that such a stamp would have been issued 50 years ago in this country. As I remember, growing up then in the American public school system, Chanukah was completely subsumed by Christmas, even in a school that had a student population that was 89% Jewish. At that time, Jews were taught — at home, in the street, and in the general society — to be relatively non-assertive about their rights, their holidays, and their place in America. But today the Jew in America is almost mainstream

America itself. Jewish politicians are being elected to major public offices in increasing numbers, even by constituencies which have few, if any, Jewish members. Even in the rarified, "old-boy-club" atmosphere of corporate America, Jews have gained entrance and prominence. Perhaps most astounding of all, many important positions in the State Department are held by Jews. In the entire history of the Exile, there has never been a situation for Jews comparable to the situation in the United States at the conclusion of the 20th century. Even the autonomous Gaonate of Babylonia and the "Golden Age" of Spanish Jewry did not approach the current integration, acceptance, and range of opportunities for Jews in our country. The Chanukah stamp is a symbol of this triumph of American Jewry, and of American society generally. Seen as such, it certainly must be reckoned as a positive development in the Jewish story in America.

But as I mentioned earlier, there is another side to the Chanukah-stamp story. The very comfort of American Jewry in its chosen home of the United States has caused a great paradox in Jewish history. The opportunity to live a full Jewish life, with full freedom of religious, educational, and cultural observance, without forfeiting any of the benefits and opportunities available to the general population, is a unique and unprecedented historical situation for Jews living outside of a Jewish state. Yet the vast majority of American Jews have chosen, most out of ignorance and some out of conscious choice, to turn their backs on their tradition. The frightening consequences of this situation are now apparent to all, with organized American Jewry now screaming in panic about "continuity." Thus, a Chanukah stamp somehow serves as a comfort to many of these otherwise disaffiliated Jews. It is exactly the type of Judaism that they are looking for — a feel-good, no-responsibility, nostalgic identity that makes no demands and defines no differences. The Chanukah stamp therefore can discharge the traditional responsibility of the menorah. It makes some

Jews proud of being Jewish without forcing them to examine the true sources and justifications for that pride. And in that sense, the Chanukah stamp may serve as a detriment to the healthy development of American Jewry.

What is truly fascinating about this paradox of the Chanukah stamp is that, in an uncanny way, it is a reflection of the original Chanukah story itself. For the struggle of the Hasmoneans was not exclusively a diplomatic and military one; it was rather a struggle for the soul of the people of Israel. Either the Jewish Hellenists were right and Jews should always accommodate themselves to the prevailing mores of the majority society, or they were so wrong that they had to be openly opposed and overcome, if not by logic, then by strength. The motto of the Hasmoneans was founded on the ancient words of Moses, who struggled himself against the Jewish apostasy of the Golden Calf: "Whoever is for G–d, let him rally to me." The Jewish Hellenists were certainly comfortable living in Greek society. They saw the Jewish Torah and way of life as being a weight around their neck, an impediment to societal acceptance and advancement. They wanted to feel good about their Judaism without having to give up their attachment to Greek ideas, behavior, and culture. They were delighted to be accepted by the dominant Greek society and did not want to risk incurring the disfavor of the Greeks in order to guarantee their own Jewish survival. A Chanukah stamp would have been more than sufficient to satisfy their Jewish guilt. Expecting the Hellenists to construct the pure menorah would have been unrealistic.

The story of Chanukah itself is illustrative of the constant, ongoing struggle of Jews to define themselves in the milieu of always-changing majority societies. The United States Postal Service has done us a greater service than it ever could have imagined by its issuance of the Chanukah stamp; for seeing the stamp focuses us on the story, paradox, and struggle of Chanukah and of the Jewish people. Apparently as it was "in those days," so is it in our time as well.

Succos

The awe and introspective contemplation of Rosh Hashanah and Yom Kippur induce a state of spiritual awakening that allows one to truly enjoy and be happy on Succos, the *festival* called "*zman simchasainu* — the time of our joy." There is a great lesson in this progression of holidays which is applicable to every facet of our lives. We are accustomed to think that joy is a spontaneous emotion, requiring no previous training, planning, or accomplishment. The holiday of Succos — the time of joy — instructs us otherwise. For without Rosh Hashanah and Yom Kippur, there would not be Succos. Without serious preparation, sacrifices of time and wealth and effort, even deprivation and fasting, joy, in Jewish terms, is not lasting and ultimately not even meaningful. Joy becomes "a good time," "a night out," something which temporarily gives us distraction, but — like drinking seawater — never really satisfies us. So we must condition ourselves to the necessity of preparation and training if we want the experience of joy to influence us in an authentic way.

A second lesson of Succos is that joy is not a singular, unique emotion that is achieved in a vacuum. The holiday of Succos has many *mitzvos* connected to it. There is the commandment regarding the *succah* (the booth constructed by Jews to eat and sleep in during the week of the holiday) itself, and there are the commandments that relate to the *esrog, lulav, hadasim,* and *aravos* (citron palm branch, myrtle which are used as part of the Succos ritual in the synagogue and home) — the four species of plants that are symbolic of G–d's bounty and blessing on this harvest festival. The synagogue service includes *hakafos* and *hoshanos* — the processions around the synagogue and the special poems composed for recitation during those processions. The *mitzvos* of Succos may be defined as joy-enhancers. They gladden and enlighten us, they make the holiday meaningful to our younger generation in a fashion that no other means of communication can approach. They provide the spiritual connection that allows our joy to be internalized and memorable, forever subject to recall and self-study. Jewish tradition knows no other form of commemorating meaningful joy except for the connection of such potentially joyful times to Torah and the G–d of Israel. Succos and its wealth of *mitzvos* make this point tellingly clear to us.

One of my lifetime dreams has been to celebrate the holiday of Succos in Jerusalem within the confines of my own *succah*. This Succos, my dream has been realized. On my beautiful balcony there stands a wonderful *succah* made of wood and canvas. And my *succah* is wonderfully furnished with a comfortable cot to sleep on, a spacious table for our family and guests, even a conversation nook to seat our drop-in guests and friends. But the finest accessory to my *succah* is Jerusalem itself. I have found that the realization of many of my dreams is somehow disappointing, because reality hardly ever lives up to fantasy. But not so when the dream is of a *succah* in Jerusalem. When a human dream is tied to a spiritual cause, to Jerusalem, to Succos, its actual realization never disappoints. For the *mitzvah* always transcends human definitions and expectations. To do a holy act, a godly deed, automatically uplifts and ennobles the one who performs. In so doing, the person is saved from the disappointment which almost always accompanies purely physical accomplishments.

This is also part of the message of Succos and helps us understand even more clearly the joy and happiness that are an integral part of this great holiday of Succos.

A Beautiful Esrog

I wish to share with you a beautiful short story about the wonderful festival of Succos. The story was authored by S.Y. Agnon, the Israeli Nobel laureate who won the prize for literature a number of years ago, and whose likeness adorns the 50-shekel note in Israeli currency. It seems that Agnon, who was born in Poland, was a neighbor of a famous old rabbi from Russia; both of them are now living in the Jerusalem neighborhood of Talpiot. One year before Succos, Agnon met his rabbinic neighbor at the neighborhood store selling *esrogim*. There Agnon noticed how meticulous his neighbor was in choosing an *esrog*. Even though he was a person of limited means, the rabbi insisted on purchasing the finest, and hence most expensive, *esrog* available. After examining many specimens, the rabbi finally chose the one he wished and paid for it. Walking home with Agnon, the rabbi emphasized to him how important it was to have a beautiful, flawless *esrog* on Succos and how the beauty of the *esrog* was part of the fulfillment of the Divine commandment for the holiday.

On Succos morning Agnon noticed that the rabbi was without an *esrog* at the synagogue services. Perplexed, Agnon asked the rabbi where his beautiful *esrog* was. The rabbi answered by relating the following incident: "I awoke early, as is my wont, and prepared to recite the blessing over the *esrog* in my *succah* located on my balcony. As you know, we have a neighbor with a large family, and our balconies adjoin. As you also know, our neighbor, the father of all these children next door, is a man of short temper. Many times he shouts at them or even hits them for violating his rules and wishes. I have spoken to him many times about his harshness but to little avail.

"As I stood in the *succah* on my balcony, about to recite the blessing for the *esrog*, I heard a child's weeping coming from the next balcony. It was a little girl crying, one of the children of our neighbor. I walked over to find out what was wrong. She told me that she too had awakened early and had gone out on her balcony to examine her father's *esrog*, whose delightful appearance and fragrance fascinated her. Against her father's instructions, she removed the *esrog* from its protective box to examine it. She unfortunately dropped the *esrog* on the stone floor, irreparably damaging it and rendering it unacceptable for ritual use. She knew that her father would be enraged and would punish her severely, perhaps even violently. Hence the frightened tears and wails of apprehension. I comforted her, and I then took my *esrog* and placed it in her father's box, taking the damaged *esrog* to my premises. I told her to tell her father that his neighbor insisted that he accept the gift of the beautiful *esrog,* and that he would be honoring me and the holiday by so doing."

Agnon concludes the story by saying: "My rabbinic neighbor's damaged, bruised, ritually unusable *esrog* was the most beautiful *esrog* I have ever seen in my lifetime."

Beauty

The festival of Succos is, among other things, the holiday of the beauty of nature. The Jews of Eastern Europe, living in poverty, squalor, and danger, and their Sephardic brothers living in the *mellahs* of the Arab countries, all consistently understated the Jewish commitment to and appreciation of the beauty and wonder of G–d's natural world. The terrible pressures of daily survival in a cruel and inimical exile dimmed the Jewish vision of beauty and natural splendor. Nevertheless, deep within the soul of Israel there remained the sense of awe and wonder regarding a Creator Who had made such a complex and marvelous universe. That recognition and appreciation of beauty is expressed in the special *mitzvos* of Succos — the *succah* itself, the four species of beautiful vegetation, the joy of the changing of the seasons, and the arrival of autumnal (or, in the southern hemisphere, spring) beauty. In fact, the holiday of Succos is called the holiday of joy and happiness due to its connection with the natural beauty of creation.

In his recent book *In Quest of G–d,* Paul Johnson, the historian/journalist, wrote as follows: "G–d, it is clear, gives us a foretaste of His beauty in the universe He has created. Its beauty, like its energizing forces, radiates from Him. Indeed, the fact that G–d rejoices in beauty is one reason why He created the universe in the first place. The universe, like G–d Himself, is living beauty, constantly changing its form with fresh delights. It creates beauty by its motions. The starry heavens were the first intimations of beauty which penetrated the minds of ... [early] men and women ... [who, though still technologically primitive] already possessed the power of ecstasy ... They grasped what beauty is about — an intimation of G–d. The stars taught them that G–d was there, and that He was even greater than the stars because He had made and arranged them and set them in motion. So beauty did indeed lead man to G–d ... There are writers, who, through their modest genius, or even by their carefully husbanded and honed talents, have sought chiefly to enable their readers to see G–d's creations with fresh eyes — have taught us to look, again and again, at the world around us and the way humans behave. To teach us about the universe, to encourage us to explore and value and treat tenderly all its manifestations and inhabitants, is a salient work of art in itself and an act of worship. Such writers are dear to G–d, and they are valuable to us too: for the understanding and reverence we bring to the world around us is a salient part of our duty, as we are beginning to discover."

The holiday of Succos aligns us with the G–d of beauty and natural wonder. It forces us to notice the perfection, complexity, and indescribable beauty of fruits and plants that we would otherwise take for granted and perhaps ignore completely. Once the *esrog* was elevated to the level of a *mitzvah*, no Jew would ever again look at the citrus fruit with callous and unfeeling eyes. And that sensitivity of understanding and appreciation of nature should spread to all of G–d's creations, whether they be human, animal, vegetable, or even inanimate mineral. It is a pathway to G–d, as all *mitzvos* are. Therefore, the prayer for rain, the greatest and most necessary gift of G–d to the natural world, is an integral part of the holiday of Succos. For rain itself is the symbol of beauty and natural sustenance in the world. Thus, all these ideas led Israel to a spirit of Succos joy in having established its relationship with the Creator of all of the natural world. The *mitzvos* of Succos should therefore continue to guide us in our own tortuous search for G–d's spirit in our own lives.

IV
CHAMPIONS

Leaders —
Born and Made

The Torah tells us of the change of leadership of the Jewish people preparatory to its entry into the Land of Israel. Moses, aware of the difficulties of leadership that 40 years of experience have taught him, turns to G–d for help in this matter of succession. His prayer is: "May the L–rd of all human spirits determine the person to lead the congregation of Israel." Moses adds that the person must be someone "who shall come before them and lead them forth and return them, so that the congregation of G–d shall not be left as a flock of sheep that has no shepherd."

Leadership is an essential ingredient for meaningful family, communal, and national life. The lack of committed and devoted leadership has sunk many a project and many a nation. One of the ills of modern society is the lack of leadership in home and family life, where many elders wish to be viewed as pals and not as parents. Communal leaders, even rabbis, often are unable to project their vision of the future effectively to their constituents and thus cannot lead them in the direction they should go. The political malaise which characterizes much of the Western democratic world today is due in large part to a perceived lack of true qualities in those leaders in whom we have placed our trust our future. It is therefore quite understandable why Moses beseeches G–d to help him in his quest for the future Jewish leader. Israel cannot be left as a "flock of sheep that has no shepherd."

You will notice that in the prayer of Moses, G–d is referred to as "the L–rd of all human spirits." Not human spirit (singular), but human spirits (plural). In this odd syntax lies the wise recognition that there is no one human spirit but that all of us are possessed of our own individual and unique spirits. A leader who does not recognize that everyone has to be treated as an individual, that everyone is entitled to his or her opinion and that it is not heresy to think differently from the leader, and that it is the leader's task to carry his flock along with his vision in spite of differing opinions and nay–sayers, is not going to be a successful leader.

To be able to be a leader for many people, who by their very human nature possess differing personalities and conflicting ideas, is the true test of leadership in a corporation, in a family, and most certainly in a nation. To survive the temptation to insist on conformity is a sign of maturity and budding greatness. Just look at the behavior of the dictators, cult leaders, and gurus of our times, and you will see the wreckage wrought by coerced conformity. The Talmud states the matter succinctly: "Just as everyone has a different face, so too does everyone possess different opinions." By this, Judaism means that just as no one is to be discarded and ridiculed for his facial appearance, neither is he to be denied his opinions. But as a corollary to this, one must realize that his opinion is always subject to the criticism and debate of others. A great leader rises above these difficulties and is able to unite the disparate personalities and ideas that are part of natural human life.

There has long existed a debate about whether one is born to leadership, or whether he can be raised and trained to become a leader. Probably both ideas are true. A leader should undertake training, education, and preparation for the task. But a leader also needs ingenuity, heart, faith, soul, and imagination. Then the people of Israel will not be a "flock of sheep without a shepherd."

"Greatness" — Real and Imagined

Greatness does not guarantee morality or goodness. Many of the people in history who entitled themselves "the great" (such as Alexander, Herod, Peter, and Catherine) were not really good people, but were rather tyrants, murderers, and profligates. There is genius and talent in evil, just as in good. The Mafia bosses, the skilled embezzlers, the computer hackers, all possess admirable skills. But bad is bad, even talented, poetic, skilled bad. In the Torah reading of *Balak* we are presented with such a talented, poetic, charismatic, skilled, *bad* person — the legendary Balaam. Balaam thus becomes the prototype for the entire genre of great people turned bad. As such, he is worthy of analysis.

Balaam's main problems are avarice, ego, and promiscuity. These are traits often recognized in people who rise to fame and power. Balaam asks a fee from Balak no less than "your entire house filled with gold and silver." His greed knows no satisfaction. As our society well knows, wealth is a narcotic, and addiction to it can prove punishing. Thus, Balaam, a potentially great man, a self-styled prophet "who knows the statements of G–d," is demeaned beyond redemption by his own greed. Balak, Balaam's client, is not fazed by the steep fee demanded of him; but Balak will never again regard Balaam as a prophet of worth. In his eyes, Balaam is now reduced to the status of a hired gun, a hatchet man, a curser. Of course, Balaam's greed is so great that he is blind to the effects of his greedy statements. In fact, in one of the great ironic statements in the Torah, Balaam describes himself as "the man with sealed eyes." He means prophecy, while the Torah means the blindness of uncontrolled avarice.

Greatness many times brings with it problems of ego. It is difficult to be "great" and humble at the same time. Moses, Hillel, and other outstanding figures of Jewish history were able to navigate the shoals of greatness and ego, but most lesser personalities find such a passage enormously difficult. Balaam is always in a state of pique, angered by imagined slights to his greatness and prowess. He is so arrogant that he brazenly attempts (and even worse, believes himself able) to hoodwink G–d. He really believes himself to be independent of G–d and man, to be above accountability for his wicked actions and venomous advice, to be above everyone and everything. This attitude of overweening pride and hubris leads to his downfall and death. But it also destroys many innocent victims in the process. Ego, when combined with avarice, is a deadly characteristic of human nature.

And, finally, Balaam's promiscuity makes him a person out of control, driven by his own inner demons to increasing levels of debasement. Even his own donkey is not safe from his deviance. There is no sense of holiness, and eventually no sense of decency and compassion, in a person whose behavior has become wanton. Balaam cannot control himself. Therefore, it is sheer folly for him to think, that he can control external events and the fate of others. Of course, one's private behavior is his own business; but in reality, a leader, an aspiring prophet, a person who demands the rewards of greatness, almost always forfeits the luxury of privacy. Balaam's greatest enemy is himself. His avarice, arrogance, and appetites all combine to make out of a man with the potential for Moses-like stature, a disgusting and ultimately empty person.

Heroes

History is replete with examples of unlikely heroes. I think that this is one of the insights into the words of king Solomon, "the race is not always to the swift, nor the battle to the mighty." The graduate chosen by classmates as being "most likely to succeed" does not always do so. And often, those who do succeed in life would certainly have been unlikely and unpredictable choices. In the Torah, the proof of this paradox lies in the story of the central human figure of Torah, our teacher Moses. A more unlikely savior and leader of Israel cannot be imagined. As an infant, Moses is left for dead, floating in the crocodile-infested waters of the Nile River, watched over only by his faithful sister, Miriam. He is saved by no one less than Batya, the daughter of Pharaoh. She, in turn, retains Moses' own mother, Jochebed, to be his wet nurse. What an unlikely chain of events! But the most unpredictable aspect of this story is that this speech-impaired, Egyptian-raised, aristocratic, and privileged young man becomes G–d's agent to redeem Israel from its centuries-long bondage in Egypt. Moses is certainly a prime example of an unlikely hero.

Throughout the Jewish experience, this phenomenon of unlikely heroes manifests itself repeatedly. The small child, Samuel, sleeping in the holy *Mishkan* (Tabernacle), near the quarters of Eli, the aged High Priest of Israel, is wakened by the spiritual voice of prophecy calling out to him while he is still only a lad. Only after Samuel presses his case on Eli a number of times does the latter finally look at him with different eyes and recognize him as the future prophet, judge, and leader of Israel. This small child, the leader of Israel? Most adults would share Eli's initial judgment of the matter — hardly! I think that this facet of unlikely and unrecognized heroism, which characterizes Samuel, is one of the bases of the Psalmist's comparison of Samuel to Moses. Eli had also previously misjudged Samuel's mother Hannah. "He thought her to be intoxicated," while she was really spiritually driven, the instrument of Providence in the salvation of Israel.

Heroes are often difficult to identify, since people are prisoners of their own prejudgments and set notions. It is ironic that Samuel himself, at the height of his prophetic and leadership powers, is guilty of leaving potential heroism and leadership unrecognized. Samuel comes to the house of Jesse to anoint a new king of Israel to replace Saul. He consistently chooses the wrong son of Jesse, and when finally instructed by Heaven to choose the youngest son, David, he is somewhat troubled and surprised. The ruddy-cheeked, fair-eyed, bold shepherd is another example of an unlikely hero, an unexpected leader. He will soon grow into the eternal king of the Jews, "the sweet singer of Israel," the hope of all humanity. What a surprise!

The problem of identifying potential greatness is a continuing and important one. How does a community choose the right leadership? In an election year, this is a crucial question. Yet there is apparently no magic formula to identify the hero and label the charlatan. How can one identify the right spouse, the correct spiritual leader, the truly good and loyal friend? Are these not the most important questions in life? By prejudging people, by using external, conformist criteria to judge others, by not looking at people in an open-minded and nonjudgmental fashion, we almost guarantee that we will miss the true hero, the potentially great leader, the "right" person for each and every one of us. In a world where such heroic people, scarce as they are, are essential for the meaningfulness of our lives, we can ill afford to overlook them.

The leader of Israel came from Pharaoh's court and not from the protected environment of the Land of Goshen. One should never prejudge Heaven's choices in these matters. It is arrogant to believe that one knows for certain how Jewish leaders should look and what their backgrounds must be. Moses, more than anyone else, proves the validity of this point of view to us.

Appreciation of Leaders

One of the central themes in the Torah deals with the death of the great leader, Aaron, the founder of the priesthood and the faithful friend and mentor of all Israel. Aaron is described in Jewish lore as being the great and magnanimous personality of Judaism, who loved the Creator, His Torah, and His people. Aaron was the peacemaker, the conciliator, the one who brought Jews closer to Torah knowledge and observance. It is therefore not remarkable that the Torah tells us that when Aaron died, the entire congregation of Israel mourned for 30 days. The Torah emphasizes the fact that "all of Israel" mourned the passing of the wonderful friend of Israel.

When Moses died, the Torah described the 30-day period of mourning in a less dramatic fashion. Rather than a sense of mourning that enveloped "all of Israel," only a portion of the society — the scholars, the judges, the true colleagues of Moses — exhibited their sense of loss and grief at the passing of the greatest leader of the Jewish people. Moses was not as close emotionally to the people as Aaron was. Moses had to do hard things. He quelled the rebellions of the Golden Calf at Sinai, of Korach and his group, of the perfidious spies and their evil view of the Land of Israel. Such leadership strength and forcefulness in a leader is necessary for the preservation of society and its moral standards. But strength of purpose and towering character rarely purchase popularity. Thus, the period of mourning for Aaron is much more emotional and widespread than the period of mourning for his brother, Moses.

Even though the depth of feeling for Aaron is certainly understandable in the light of his personality and popularity among the people of Israel, the Rabbis of the Midrash saw in the more muted mourning for Moses a slight lack of appreciation for the great leader. It was as though the Jewish people were not really appreciative of Moses and did not assess his greatness as accurately as they should have. Aaron was beloved, the holy man whom everyone admired, but he was not faced with the terrible decisions of leadership that constantly beset Moses. Without Moses there could be no Jewish people. The Jewish people should have realized this basic fact and treated Moses with the appreciation that his role and contribution deserved.

When Joshua dies, the *Tanach* makes no mention of any extended period of mourning by Israel. The Rabbis commented again that the people of Israel were endangered because of G–d's displeasure with them for their lack of appreciation of the greatness and leadership of Joshua during his long career of public service. In the words of the Rabbis, the name of the burial place of Joshua, described in *Tanach* as being "north of the mountain volcano," indicates the wrath — the dormant volcano of G–d's justice and retribution — against Israel for its lack of thankfulness to and appreciation of Joshua during his lifetime and especially at his death. It is no wonder, therefore, that after the death of Joshua and his colleagues, the "elders of Israel," the Jewish people sank into anarchy, idolatry, and immorality. They abandoned the traditions of Moses, Aaron, and Joshua and rejected the G–d of Israel. They no longer appreciated what had been done for them in the past, nor those who labored for them.

People who are unappreciative of others, of parents, teachers, public leaders, eventually become unappreciative of their Creator as well. Judaism has always been built on the basis of appreciation for everything we have — people, our great past, and the G–d of Israel. Only such an attitude can guarantee our future.

V
ON THE ROAD

A Summer
in Provence

In 1165, the intrepid Jewish traveler of the Middle Ages, Benjamin of Tudela, journeyed from Toledo, Spain, to the part of southern France known as Provence. In his diary, which has survived till today, Benjamin records his impressions of the Jewish communities of that area, their scholars and leaders, their disputes and problems, and their greatness and vitality. I was always fascinated by Benjamin's travelogue, and I hoped for an opportunity to retrace his route through Provence myself. Through the grace of American Airlines' Advantage Frequent Flyer Miles Program, my long-suffering wife's forbearance with my schemes, and a great air-conditioned, six-cylinder Citroen rental car, I was able to realize my dream this past summer.

After arriving in Paris, clearing customs quickly (I have an honest face), and receiving our rental car, we immediately set out for Lyon, which is the gateway to Provence coming from the north. Provence is very hot in the summer, with a climate and a look much like Israel's. No wonder the Jews of Provence felt so much at home there. The temperature during summer days in Provence is always in the 90s and many times goes over 100. An air-conditioned car is not a luxury, but rather a necessity. The definition of air conditioning in the hotels of Provence (even four-star ones) is not the same as it is in the United States. It must be the language barrier, but I would estimate the difference between U.S. air conditioning and Provencal air conditioning to be 15 degrees on the side of heat. But, as my Talmud *rebbe* said many decades ago, "Where is it written that education must be air conditioned?" And Provence is certainly an education for Jews willing to explore it.

Provence is a history buff's paradise. There are monumental relics from Roman times. The great Roman bridge and aqueduct at Nimes, the Pont du Gard, defies description and even imagination. The Roman theater at Oranger, with the statue of Augustus with his sightless marble eyes overlooking the scene, is still intact and in use. The opposition of the rabbis of the Talmud to Roman theaters is well understood in viewing the remnants of the paganism, debauchery, and violence that marked every presentation there. The temple to Jupiter in Arles, built by Augustus, to honor his grandsons, stands mute, empty, and lifeless. The amphitheaters that witnessed the slaughter of so many innocent humans are still in use in Provence. Some of them, especially those close to the Spanish border, now witness the slaughter of bulls and the occasional matador, while others are used for concerts and theatrical presentations.

The Roman legions and settlers in Provence were accompanied by Jews who served as suppliers to the Roman armies and eventually as merchants, tradespeople, and artisans. This first Jewish settlement in Provence, which began approximately in the year 50 B.C.E., ended five centuries later with the collapse of Roman rule and the beginning of the Dark Ages. There are no vestiges of Jewish life from that period apparent today, though I had an eerie feeling throughout my visit of having been in Provence before. So much for the supernatural.

The Jews reappeared in Provence in the 10th and 11th centuries. The famed Rabbi Moshe HaDarshan (the Preacher) lived in Narbonne and was one of the founders of medieval Provencal Jewry. Rashi, in his own commentary to the Bible, often quotes interpretations and commentaries on the Bible advanced by Rabbi Moshe. In a later time, Narbonne was home to the famous father-and-son scholars, Rabbis Yosef and David Kimchi (Radak). Rabbi Manoach of Narbonne wrote a famous commentary to *Mishnah Torah* of Rambam. Yet there is no Jewish life in Narbonne today. It is a sleepy town with almost no remembrance of the role it once played in Jewish life and scholarship. However, as in almost all Provence, there is a street or town square that bears a "Jewish" association. In order to find these "Jewish" streets, one should repair, ironically, to the area of the oldest and largest church in town. Invariably, leading off of that church square, there will be a small, narrow, sometimes even partially covered medieval street, called "Rue Hebraique" or "Rue Jerusalem" or "Rue Juifs." One can then walk down that street, still flanked by buildings of the 12th and 13th centuries that are still in use, and feel the hallowed footsteps of our great ancestors whose devotion to Torah and Judaism still sparks Jewish scholarship today. To me, it was a moving and emotional moment to literally walk in the footsteps of Rabbi Moshe HaDarshan, Radak, and others. History is not only facts, dates, and knowledge. It is also dreams, imagination, emotion, a feeling of bonding beyond place and time. Every time I see Rabbi Moshe HaDarshan's or Radak's commentaries now, I feel an affinity with them and I find myself smiling a warm and respectful smile of recognition and empathy.

The oldest Jewish relics in Provence are in Carpentras. There one sees a synagogue building built in 1741, on the foundation of a 12th-century synagogue. The *matzah* bakery and the *mikvah* (ritual bath) in the basement of the building are from medieval times. There is also a large bare room downstairs that may have served as the *taharah* (ritual purification) room for preparing Jewish bodies for burial. By the way, no Jewish cemeteries have survived in Provence from the Middle Ages. The *bimah* or *tebah* (stage) from which the Torah was read is on a mezzanine level overhanging the men's section of the synagogue. The women's sections are located on both sides of the main men's section, but are some five feet lower than it. There is a beautiful miniature seat of Elijah in the niche of the east wall of the synagogue. There are no Jews in Carpentras, and the synagogue is shown by a French woman obviously bored by the whole thing. The enormity of the emptiness and loneliness of the Jewish exile is an ever constant companion to one who tours Jewish Provence.

The main Jewish community in medieval Provence was Lunel. Jews who came from there proudly used the name *Ha-Yarchi* (from the moon, *Lunel* meaning moon in Provencal French) to identify themselves as Lunelites. There lived Rabbi Yehonasan HaKohen, the correspondent of Maimonides, Rabbi Zerachyah HaLevi, the Baal HaMaor (writer of a famous Talmudic and halachic text), Rabbis Samuel and Yehuda ibn Tibon, the translators of Maimonides' Arabic works into Hebrew, Rabbi Avraham Beis Din (Ravad II), the father-in-law of Ravad III of Posquieres (a town in Provence which no longer exists), Rabbi Avraham ben Nosson (Ravon), the author of the famous Talmudic work *HaManhig*, and many other great scholars and teachers of Israel. This city of great Jewish history, whose scholars are still engaged in lively debate and discussion in every yeshivah in the modern-day world, has no Jews. Yet, as in Narbonne, walking its Jewish street can mist one's eyes.

The city of Montpellier houses the oldest medical college in all of Europe. Founded in the 12th century by Jewish and Moslem doctors from Spain, it still operates today as a school of humanity and healing. In Montpellier one may see *mikvaos* (ritual baths) from the 13th century under the old city walls. The

Jews of Montpellier identified themselves by the use of the name *Min HaHar* (from the mountain, a derivative of the French *Montpellier*).

There are also Jewish relics in the towns of L'Isle sur Sorgue, Pernes les Fontaines, Cavaillon, Trets, Aix en Provence, Saint Remy de Provence, and Tarascon. Provence is pervaded by Jewish memories, and the golden sun of that province evokes the shadows of former Jewish glory. There are major Jewish communities today in Montpellier, Avignon, and Marseilles. These communities are from the post-World War II era and are composed mainly of Sephardic Jews who emigrated from North Africa to France when Algeria, Morocco, and Tunisia became independent states. The assimilation of these Jews into French society has unfortunately been rapid and almost complete.

Finally, I want to tell you of the walled city of Avignon. There the schismatic popes of France in the 14th century resided and built an enormous papal palace. There is a reception hall the size of a football field where the pope greeted visitors. There is only one chair at the end of the room, naturally for the pope, with everyone else constantly required to stand. The pope's bedroom, though ornate, feels uncomfortable. He never slept alone but always had two priests in the room with him who would wake him every three hours for prayers. The city of Avignon had a Jewish population who were the "pope's Jews." Legend has it that these Jews actually met in the basement rooms of the papal palace for prayer and study! Avignon is one of the most interesting places in Provence, if not in all of Europe.

Knowledge of French is helpful but not necessarily essential for a trip through Provence, but some background on its history and a lively imagination will definitely help.

Cracow and Lublin

The 50th year of the liberation of the death camps at Auschwitz/Birkenau and the controversial commemorations that marked the event reminded me of the great beginnings of Polish Jewry in the 15th and 16th centuries. At that time, Jewish life in Poland was centered in two major cities, Cracow and Lublin. Throughout Polish history these two cities were the royal cities of Torah in Poland. Even though Warsaw would become the city with the largest Jewish population in Poland in the 19th and 20th centuries, Cracow and Lublin jealously guarded their primacy in the lives of Polish Jews.

Cities are known mainly because of the great people who lived and flourished there. The story of Cracow, in Jewish mind and soul, is therefore inextricably associated with the great Rabbi Moses Isserles (*Rema*) who was its spiritual leader in the 16th-century. The story of Lublin is also bound to the great personages of its 16th century rabbinic leaders, Rabbis Solomon Luria (*Maharshal*) and Meir (*Maharam*) of Lublin, as well as to its 20th-century scholar and head, Rabbi Meir Shapiro. All of these great men bear study and analysis.

Rabbi Moses Isserles was born in Cracow in 1530. He traveled to Lublin in early adolescence, there to become the main disciple and eventually the son-in-law of Rabbi Shalom Shachna, the dean of the major yeshivah then existing in Poland. Rabbi Moses was a person of genius and piety, soft spoken, genial, modest, and beloved by all. At the age of 21 he was already one of the judges sitting on the major *bais din* (court) in Cracow. He soon was acknowledged as the leading legal authority in Cracow, and his fame spread throughout

Poland, eventually reaching the entire Jewish world. Though plagued by tragedy in his personal life, he nevertheless always exhibited a demeanor of faith, serenity, and unwavering optimism to his community of Cracow, which relied upon him in all matters, public and private, communal and personal.

Rabbi Moses was well versed in worldly knowledge, mathematics, astronomy, and philosophy. He understood people; he sought to reconcile and not divide. He was a follower of Maimonides but nevertheless defended Ashkenazic Jewry's customs and halachic decisions even when they differed from his mentor's opinions. When the Sephardic scholar Rabbi Yosef Caro published his *Shulchan Aruch* and proclaimed it to be the repository of Torah law for all of Israel, Rabbi Moses Isserles introduced his own glosses and terse comments into the text of the work itself, thereby preserving the integrity and authority of the *Shulchan Aruch* and at the same time reconciling its decisions with Ashkenazic thought and practice. He was the architect of harmony in the Jewish world.

Rabbi Moses Isserles died in 1572, on the auspicious day of Lag B'Omer (18 Iyar), and was buried in the old Jewish cemetery of Cracow. His grave became a shrine for much of Polish Jewry for centuries, and tens of thousands of Polish Jews made their way to his monument every Lag B'Omer. Legend credited him with living 33 years (actually 42 years), authoring 33 major books of scholarship, and dying on the 33rd day of the Omer. The love of Polish Jewry for this gentle giant of Torah scholarship knew no bounds. In today's Cracow, a city almost *Judenrein* and not far from the sinister smokestacks of Auschwitz/Birkenau, his small chapel still remains, as does his grave. But more importantly, his influence and leadership still exist, unabated and undiminished, everywhere in the Jewish world 423 years after his passing.

If Cracow was the seat of serenity and reconciliation, Lublin was more representative of the feisty and argumentative nature that was typical of Polish Jewry. The rabbi of Lublin in the middle of the 16 century was the aforementioned Rabbi Shalom Shachna. He was famous for his pilpulistic method of Talmudic study, a dialectical study approach using wide-ranging comparisons, and imaginative and sometimes circuitous reasoning. He was the official Chief Rabbi of Poland, having been appointed to this powerful post by the Polish king.

In Lublin at that time, occupying a lesser rabbinic position, was Rabbi Solomon Luria. A genius and scholar of immense proportions, he was the author of a noted commentary on a number of major tractates of the Talmud as well as on a series of illuminating notes on the entire Talmud, and he also au-thored a major work dealing with the laws of kosher food. Strong minded and independent, he brooked no compromises on matters he considered fundamental to correct methods of Torah study and Jewish jurisprudence. He disagreed openly with Rabbi Shalom Shachna over the correctness of pilpulistic study. He disputed the right of Rabbi Yosef Caro to establish the *Shulchan Aruch* as the basic law book of Israel, claiming that it would lead to a lowering of scholarly standards in matters of halachic decision. He criticized Rabbi Moses Isserles (who was a distant relative of his) for his tolerance of the study of phi-losophy and for defending certain Ashkenazic customs which he felt were improper. Nevertheless, his penchant for truth led him to eulogize Rabbi Moses Isserles with these words: "From Moses (Maimonides) to Moses (Isserles) there arose none like Moses (*Rema*)." When he died on 12 Kislev 1574, he was rec-ognized as one of the great Talmudists of all time, a throwback to the age of the great scholars of the House of Rashi (from whom he was descended) and one of the pillars of the house of Polish Jewry.

Rabbi Meir of Lublin was born in 1558. He maintained a large yeshivah in Lublin. True to his Polish heritage, he was loyal to the pilpulistic style of Talmudic study, but in nature and tem-perament he was close to Rabbi Solomon Luria, the great opponent of *pilpul*. Rabbi Meir was already the head of the yeshivah in Lublin when he was only 24 years old. Because of his fiery nature and the resulting controversies in which he was involved, he left Lublin in 1587 and became the head of the yeshivah in Cracow. However, Cracow could not hold the turbulent Rabbi Meir, and in 1595 he left Cracow to become the rabbi of Lvov. There he was embroiled in a series of bitter disputes. He finally resigned the rabbinic position of Lvov and returned to Lublin, there to live out his remaining days. He was the author of a series of famous glosses on the entire Talmud, as well as books of responsa. He is also famous for his formulation of the formal "*heter iska*," the legal mechanism by which a loan between Jews is transformed into a business investment, thus allowing profits (interest) to be paid to the investor (lender). In his death, *Maharam* of Lublin achieved the appreciation and recognition of Israel for his Torah greatness, which had escaped him for much of his life, and he is reckoned as the third main pillar upon which the Jewish community of 16th-century Poland was built.

The last great rabbinic figure of Lublin was Rabbi Meir Shapiro, who died in 1933. He built the first great modern yeshivah in Poland, Yeshivah Chachmei Lublin. This yeshivah was the crown of Polish Jewry in the years between the terrible wars of the 20th century. A great orator and organizer, creative, innovative, and tireless, he was the outstanding spokesman for traditional Jewry in Poland. He was a member of the Polish *sejm* (parliament) and active in all Jewish affairs. His visits to the United States did a great deal to help strengthen Jewish life in the New World in the 1920s. His untimely death at the age of 44 plunged Polish and world Jewry into shock and mourning. The great building of Yeshiva Chachmei Lublin still stands in Lublin, a sad testimony to the unbelievable and cruel end of Polish Jewish life. One can say regarding the Jewish community of Lublin, paraphrasing *Maharshal's* appraisal of *Rema*: "From Meir (*Maharam* of Lublin) to Meir (Shapiro), there arose no one like Meir (Rabbi Meir Shapiro, the rabbi of Lublin)".

Polish Jewry will eventually be remembered not through Auschwitz, Majdanek, or Chelmno but rather through Cracow and Lublin. For the spirit, knowledge, and contributions of the great men of Jewish Poland over the centuries still inspire and strengthen all. The legacy of Polish Jewry to the entire Jewish people remains today vital and necessary, always important and eternally young and fresh.

Hong Kong and the Jewish Problem

During mid-March 1996, my wife and I were able to visit Hong Kong, where I was invited to deliver a number of lectures to the local Jewish community. The entire community of Hong Kong is fascinating and exotic to Western eyes, and the Jewish community is also fascinating and exotic.

To begin with, Hong Kong is a long, long way from the United States. The non stop flight from Los Angeles lasts over $15\frac{1}{2}$ hours. Therefore, the choice of airlines is an important factor. Our Hong Kong hosts strongly recommended flying with the Hong Kong airline. They assured us that the difference in comfort and service afforded by this Asian airline over an American carrier was one of kind and not merely degree. They did not exaggerate. The flight attendants are from a variety of Asian countries, but the common denominator among them is their atmosphere of serenity, their spirit of service, their attention to detail, and their unobtrusive omnipresence. But in spite of all the comforts and amenities of the airline, it is a very long flight and it feels like it.

The Pacific Ocean is limitless in size and scope. I am reminded of the comment made by the head of the American naval division of convoys in the Pacific Ocean during the Second World War, explaining the lack of success of Japanese submarine warfare against American shipping: "It is a big ocean and the convoys are small dots, easily able to remain undiscovered in the vastness of the waters." Flying across the Pacific Ocean, seeing nothing but water for hours on end, gives one a perspective regarding G–d's world and its wonders. It is no wonder that Jewish tradition requires one to recite a special blessing of wonderment and awe when viewing this great ocean.

Hong Kong is a very exciting place, and the excitement begins with the landing approach toward the current airport serving Hong Kong. The pilot announced in his soothing voice and clipped British accent that we would make a "splendidly sharp" right turn over Hong Kong harbor and land *between* the very tall apartment buildings that line the approach to the runway, which is the only active one at the airport. It is an eerie feeling to see people looking down at you from their apartment windows while you are sitting in an enormous 747 landing on this small spit of land in Hong Kong harbor.

My first and most lasting impression of Hong Kong after landing was one of amazement at the sheer number of people present on this small piece of land. The population of Hong Kong is six million, and the press of so many people living in dense proximity to one another affects every aspect of Hong Kong life. Almost one-quarter of the earth's population is Chinese, and the potential power and global influence of this immense population often escapes Westerners. One visit to Hong Kong will be sufficient to impress the reality of that population on anyone's mind. There are numerous levels of sidewalks in central Hong Kong in order to accommodate pedestrian traffic, which otherwise would be in a constant state of deadlock. On a rainy day — and there are many of them in

Hong Kong — the forest of umbrellas further impedes the flow of traffic. Nevertheless, everyone somehow seems to arrive at his destination, though it does require alacrity, ingenuity, and perseverance.

One of the innovations perfected in Hong Kong to help keep pedestrian traffic moving is the "escalator." This Rube Goldberg-type contraption is a series of escalators, moving sidewalks, and "stations" that allows pedestrians to proceed to the Central area from Mid-levels and vice versa. The "escalator" runs in one direction only at any given time — down to Central for four hours in the morning and up towards Mid-levels the rest of the day. Noted halachic authorities who have visited Hong Kong and inspected the operation of the "escalator" closely are of the opinion that it may be used on the Sabbath and Jewish holidays. However, I noted that some of the observant Jews in Hong Kong eschewed the use of the "escalator" on the Sabbath, perhaps as a statement of personal piety, or perhaps for the more mundane reason that it was running in the wrong direction for them at that time. In any event, the city is so crowded, busy, and noisy, constantly and unendingly, its atmosphere of commerce and work so intense and all-pervasive, that I found it difficult to establish an internal Sabbath atmosphere for myself outside the holy confines of the synagogue. Perhaps since I came from rural Monsey and no autos are seen on our streets on the Sabbath, I found this oppressively urban scene difficult to adjust to.

The Jewish community in Hong Kong is more than a century old. Its origins lie in Jews from Iraq and Syria who moved to India and followed the British Raj to Hong Kong at the end of the 19th century. These Sephardic Jewish families, involved in every possible trade activity imaginable, found Hong Kong to be a lucrative and challenging location. A number of these Jewish families became the founding families of English Hong Kong itself, becoming fabulously wealthy, influential, and assimilated in the process. The electric power station, the

main tunnel connecting Hong Kong island to Kowloon penin-
sula and the mainland, large tracts of Hong Kong real estate,
as well as many important commercial establishments, hotels,
and retail trades are or were owned by these prominent Jewish families. The permanent Jewish community in Hong Kong
currently numbers about 2,500 people, a significant number
of them Israeli expatriates. There are always many Jewish
business people from all over the world in Hong Kong, and
there are also a number of Jewish tourists. The Jewish community is therefore varied and multicultured at all times. I saw
Chasidic Jews wearing their *shtreimels* on the streets of Hong
Kong on the Sabbath, as well as black-hatted Jews, *kippah*-
wearing Jews, and bareheaded Jews coming to the
synagogues. Since Jews are such a minute percentage of the
overall population (2,500 people out of a total of 6 million residents!), the general population apparently does not even
notice the Jew on the street. The fact that Hong Kong is such
a cosmopolitan city, with Filipinos, Indians, Thais, and other
ethnic groups always swarming in great numbers on its
streets, also serves to mask any general impression of Jewish
presence in its society.

In 1902 the main synagogue, Ohel Leah, was constructed in
Mid-levels. A small gem of a building, it is built in the style of
the synagogues that once graced Bombay and Calcutta. Its interior is completely Sephardic in design, and its Holy Ark and
Scrolls of the Law (*sifrei Torah*) are of Sephardic appearance
and tradition. In fact, the physical appearance and ambience of
the synagogue, as well as the style and character of its prayer
services, reminded me greatly of the synagogues in Avignon
and Nice in southern France that I attended a number of sum-
mers ago. Ohel Leah is an Orthodox congregation with an
Orthodox rabbi from the United States. It remains today as the
main synagogue in Hong Kong, but it is by no means the only
congregation there. There is a Chabad congregation, also headed by an American rabbi, whose venue is located in a major

hotel in central Hong Kong. This congregation has as its nucleus a number of permanent Hong Kong families, many of whom have become more observant over time due to the influence of that local Chabad rabbi. Also, most observant Jewish businessmen and tourists staying in the hotels in central Hong Kong naturally attend this Chabad synagogue out of convenience or preference.

There is a third Orthodox congregation composed mainly of Syrian and Iraqi Jews, headed by a Sephardic rabbi from Israel, located in Kowloon on the mainland. Though this congregation is relatively new and small in numbers, it shows promise of success and has been able to attract some of the former Israelis of Sephardic descent who feel somewhat uncomfortable with American Ashkenazic rabbis. There are also a number of young Orthodox American families that are in Hong Kong on temporary assignment from their employers. They have begun to be active in the local Jewish community, even though they have terrible pangs of homesickness. I have found that the Americans the world over always lend a positive flavor to their surroundings.

One thing gave me pause on my visit to Hong Kong. I knew both the Chabad and Ohel Leah rabbis during their youth in Chicago, I remembered them as teen-age yeshivah students and now I saw them decades later as mature leaders of a Jewish community. Am I really that old? I don't feel that old (thank G–d), but the evidence of the passage of time is incontrovertible. It was also very interesting to me that the old rapport that I had with them long ago in Chicago had somehow survived the years and the continents. I also thought how unlikely it would have seemed to all three of us decades ago in Chicago that we would meet again on a project of Jewish education in faraway Hong Kong. The L–rd and His ways are pretty much inscrutable.

There is a small Jewish day school operating in Hong Kong. Founded only a few years ago, it now has four classes and a school population of approximately 65. There is also a series of weekly classes in Torah for high-school-age Jewish students who attend some of the fine private (French, English, American, etc.) schools in Hong Kong. Amazingly enough, a number of young people, upon their graduation from high school, have left for a year or two years' study in Torah schools in Israel. As in most small Jewish communities in the world, children who receive an intensive Torah education rarely return to settle in those small communities where they were born and raised. The annexation of Hong Kong by China is also a very dampening factor, negating any practical reason for these young people to return and help build the Hong Kong Jewish community. Thus, the Jewish community, with all of its wealth and tradition, apparently faces strangulation and extinction by attrition.

Hong Kong faces an uncertain future. China's annexation of Hong Kong took place in July of 1997. In its transference agreement with the English, China committed itself to the maintenance of the political and economic status quo of Hong Kong for the next 50 years. All logic seems to dictate that it would be in China's own best interests to honor that agreement and maintain Hong Kong as the commercial center that it now is. However, the world and the behavior of its governments do not usually conform to logic or even long-term beneficial self-interest. When I was in Hong Kong, China was daily launching armed missiles into the Straits of Taiwan in a blatant attempt to intimidate the island's government and influence the results of its impending elections. China's behavior cast a palpable pall over the daily life of Hong Kong, for it communicated clearly the unwillingness of China to countenance the presence of a dynamic, capitalistic, Western-oriented, relatively democratic society and government on its doorstep, lest it contaminate by example the surviving dinosaur of Communism which is present-day China. If China feels that way about Taiwan, then how will it act towards Hong Kong now that it has assumed control of the area? All that Hong Kong has achieved, after all, stands as an implicit indictment of the Communist government and society of China and its record of social, human, and economic failures.

In an article that appeared recently in *The New York Times*, Mark Roberti wrote: "Although there has never been great hope that Beijing will accept democracy [in ruling Hong Kong], it has repeatedly promised not to interfere with the colony's vibrant economy. However, its decision [currently announced] to treat non-Chinese [residents] differently [from native Hong Kong Chinese] threatens to erode Hong Kong's status as an international business center. One reason Hong Kong has developed into Asia's leading commercial and financial center is that it not only welcomes foreign companies, it also welcomes immigrants, especially those with capital ... These non-Chinese immigrants have played an important role in building Hong Kong by forgoing international links and bringing in foreign technology and management techniques. Now, they have no idea what their future will be. For those who have decided not to leave, Beijing's actions suggest that China is prepared to sacrifice them and their international ties for the sake of controlling Hong Kong's population ... Like Beijing's plans to scrap the elected legislature and Bill of Rights, the decision to treat non-Chinese permanent residents differently could seriously injure Hong Kong's political and economic future."

The real point of Chinese logic, like that of all totalitarian regimes, is to retain absolute power and control over its groaning subjects. All other conventional Western democratic logic — economics, prestige, world opinion, practical benefits, and technological advancements — pale into nothingness when measured against the dictator's need to control and terrorize a subservient population. That has been the lesson of our century many times over, and it appears that poor, wealthy Hong Kong will soon be the victim of this lesson as well.

All of the Jews that I spoke to are "sitting on the suitcases." They are waiting to see what the reality of Chinese rule will look like. They all possess foreign passports and have attempted to develop escape plans for themselves and their fortunes. It is ironic, therefore, that the Hong Kong Jewish community, like that of South Africa, is more vibrantly Jewish now than perhaps ever before in its history, at a time when it is most politically vulnerable and its future very uncertain. Long-time Jewish Hong Kong residents are either leaving and planning to leave, and this is a destabilizing fact of life in the Jewish community. A further irony is that the Jewish community as a whole is wealthy beyond imagination. It sits on a trust fund of many tens of millions of dollars, the result of the sale of property at enormous prices a number of years ago. The money is to be spent exclusively on the institutions of the Hong Kong Jewish community. Thus, there is a real opportunity to build and even to import personnel who would devote themselves to the creation and maintenance of schools, yeshivas, social welfare agencies, and other communal organizations. A magnificent Jewish community center has recently been built. The center contains within it a lovely glatt-kosher restaurant that serves the local Jewish community as well as all of the Jewish tourists and visitors in Hong Kong. It also houses a library, private dining rooms, lecture hall, health club, and other amenities. However, all of this wealth and opportunity has validity only if there is a Jewish community. And the likelihood of having such a community in Hong Kong decades from now is certainly questionable, if not doubtful. But the Orient is inscrutable: No one really knows what the future of Hong Kong and its Jews will be.

On the Oregon Trail

n November 1996, I lectured in Portland and Eugene,
Oregon, on successive nights. Both cities have fledgling
Orthodox communities, though Portland's synagogue
and community dates back to 1905, while Eugene's "Halachic Minyan" synagogue is only about one year old.
Both communities are blessed with newly arrived, young, talented, energetic rabbinic couples, who, by the force of their
personalities and unremitting efforts, have already begun to
change the tenor of Jewish life in Oregon. As a token of my
visit, I was presented with a copy of a book entitled *The Jews
of Oregon — 1850-1950*.

On the long flight back to New York, I had an opportunity to
skim the book, and I found it to be a fascinating one. The story
of the Jews of Oregon is a microcosm of the story of the Jews
in America generally. As such, it is an instructive historical
saga.

As early as 1844, there was a Jewish presence in Oregon. A
decade later, the Jewish community in Portland was already established. The Jews in Oregon at that time were almost
exclusively German, mostly from Bavaria. They were a mixture
of Reform and more traditional Jews, and the first congregation
in Portland, Congregation Beth Israel, was founded in 1858. Its
constitution declared its purpose: "To organize a congregation
for the worship of the One, only, everlasting G–d, according to
the ancient ritual of the Jewish Faith." But the congregants
could never agree on how this noble purpose was to be accom-
plished. The congregation was badly split between the followers
and believers in Reform — and Reform in the 1850s in America was very radical — and the more traditional Jews, who,
though perhaps personally lax in observance of the tenets of

Judaism, demanded that their synagogue conform to traditional standards. Any rabbi hired during the first decade of the congregation's existence was forced into resignation by this internal strife.

In 1869, the situation was finally resolved in the time-honored, typical fashion — the congregation split into two. Beth Israel became a Reform temple, and the traditionalists formed another synagogue ironically called Ohavei Shalom, "The Lovers of Peace." A radical Reform rabbi, Mayer May, the disciple of Isaac Mayer Wise, the founder of American Reform, was elected as the new rabbi of Beth Israel. But his agenda was so radical that he soon found himself enmeshed in great controversy even among his Reform congregants. May actually fired a gun at one of his chief congregational tormentors and was finally forced to resign.

With the arrival in Portland of immigrants from Eastern Europe, Orthodox synagogues were organized and built. Talmud Torah Neve Zedek, Shaarei Torah, and Kesser Israel were the first congregations. Shaarei Torah still survives as a major congregation, though it is no longer strictly Orthodox and apparently plans to join the Conservative movement in the near future. Kesser Israel, however, remains strictly Orthodox, housed in its original 90-year-old building along with all of the traditions that are ensconced therein. But it has a new young rabbi, an enthusiastic group of young couples that have revitalized the congregation, and a Torah-learning program that will undoubtedly pay great dividends for the survival and growth of Portland Jewry. It will not be an easy task, however, for Kesser Israel to succeed. Decades of inactivity, neglect, and lack of spirit and hope for the future are not erased in a few years, no matter how great the effort the new group exerts, and no matter how devoted and talented they are. And the plight of Kesser Israel and Portland certainly is reflective of the entire American Jewish scene. It's going to be a long haul for the Jewish community to extricate itself from centuries of neglect and false idols and ideals, but I feel the momentum building for a revival of Torah values is now present, perhaps for the first time in two centuries.

An inveterate tourist, I took some time in Portland to visit the natural wonders of the breathtaking Oregon-Washington Pacific Northwest. The fact that it rained a monsoon both days that I was in there only redoubled my determination to do some sight-seeing of the wonders of nature that are easily accessible by car. The Mount Saint Helens Park Visitor Center is a must-see place. There is a film of the eruption of this active volcano a number of years ago, which gives renewed meaning to the word "awesome." The entire exhibition regarding that volcanic erup-tion, which includes a slide-show, a diorama made to scale, numerous outstanding photographs, and other memorabilia of that fateful day when the mountain blew its top, is riveting. The beauty of the mountains and forests, even in the rain and with low clouds hiding the high peaks of the Cascade mountain range, is a balm to the spirit and soul of a jaded New Yorker. What a religious and emotional experience it is to find oneself in the midst of the gigantic wonders of G–d's nature!

I also traveled to the Bonneville Dam over the mighty Co-lumbia River. The dam is named after a captain in the United States Army who helped chart major portions of the Oregon Trail in the early 1800s. It is a majestic structure, almost fright-ening in its size and scope. Driving over the top of the dam, with the great river coursing under you and ocean-going freighters being raised and lowered in the locks that are part of the dam compound, one becomes aware of the genius and magnitude of the imaginative scope of human beings. The system of locks dates back to 1896, but the major Bonneville Lock, which is the key to the navigability of the Columbia River, was completed only in 1938. The newest and largest lock, incorporating all modern technological advances in the field, was opened for traffic in 1993. This lock does the work of seven previous locks that were located upstream, and it has cut over three hour's time from the journey across the Columbia River from upriver to its Pacific Ocean mouth.

But the most fascinating exhibit at the Bonneville Dam, at least to me, is the fish ladder which allows millions of salmon to wend their way through the obstacle of the dam without being mashed in the turbines of its great hydro-electric project. Fish ladders are the passageways for adult fish that migrate upstream seasonally on the Columbia River. Pools in the fish ladders are formed by cross barriers (weirs) that form steps, set in a ramp leading up to and around the dam. The cross barriers have openings along the bottom to allow the fish to swim easily from one stairstep to the next. Chinook, coho, and sockeye salmon, as well as steelhead, shad, and other fish, use the ladders in their upstream migration. Between 700,000 and one million upstream migrant adult salmon and steelhead, and from 30 to 50 million downstream migrant salmon and steelhead fingerlings (baby fish), pass Bonneville Dam every year. There is a fish-viewing window at the dam where one can actually see the fish on their way up or down the Columbia River, and there is also an official fish-counter, paid for by our taxes, who sits near the window and actually counts every fish that swims by.

I also saw some of the most magnificent, fragile, delicate waterfalls that it has ever been my pleasure to observe on the road back from Bonneville Dam to Portland. It is a very dangerous road to drive upon because the scenery is so spectacular that it is terribly distracting. There are, however, many look-out points that allow drivers to pull off the road, park, and absorb the beauty of G–d's unspoiled world. It is almost always the tourist and sightseer, however, who pulls off the road to admire the mountains, the forest, the waterfalls, and the roaring river; the average Oregonian, harassed and busy, stressed and driven, as all of us are (well, maybe a little less so than his New York-based fellow countryman), apparently hardly notices his surroundings and certainly takes them for granted. But as for me, the magnificence of the natural beauty of the Pacific Northwest alone vindicates the trek across the American continent to witness it. I was most gratified to have been able to make my way across the Oregon Trail and to share my impressions of it with you.

A South African Interlude

My wife and I were in South Africa during a good portion of the month of February 1997. February in South Africa is the August of the Northern Hemisphere, and as such, the warm, sunny days there were a welcome respite from the dreariness of a New York winter. South Africa must be one of the most scenic, beautiful, and temperate locations on our earth. The city of Capetown is most supremely endowed with all of the wonders that bays, two oceans, mountains, and perfect weather can bestow. We visited Durban, the port on the Indian Ocean, which reminded us of our years in Miami Beach, with its semitropical climate and beach resorts. Most of our stay was in Johannesburg, the capital of the country and the city that contains the largest Jewish population in Africa. We were also treated to a two-day photographic safari visit to Kruger National Park, a natural game reserve near the Mozambique border. The park is larger than the state of Massachusetts and is populated by lions, cheetahs, elephants, crocodiles, Cape buffalo, hyenas, wild dogs, warthogs, impala, giraffes, wildebeest, springbok, eagles, hippopotami, rhinceros, zebras, ostriches, baboons, and open Land Rovers bearing goggle-eyed humans. There are also malaria-carrying mosquitoes present, and any visit to the park requires the use of prophylactic antimalaria drugs before, during, and after the stay. But the experience of Kruger National Park and, in fact, of South Africa generally, is an unforgettable and fascinating one.

This was not the first trip to South Africa for my wife and me. We had visited South Africa 12 years ago and again 10 years ago. As you can well imagine, the new South Africa led by Nelson Mandela is a far different nation from the country dominated by the apartheid ideology of the previous Afrikaaner-run society. And while most of the change is undoubtedly positive in the long run, especially for the tens of millions of blacks who form the vast majority of the population, there are many disturbing new signs of the potentially dangerous underlying problems that face South Africa.

The problem that is most openly discussed and which occupies a great deal of space in the daily newspapers and other media is that of crime, both organized and random. Car-jackings are a daily, if not hourly, occurrence in Johannesburg. People live in wonderful homes, surrounded by lush gardens, swimming pools, and pleasant, considerable neighbors. But they also are surrounded by high, spiked walls which are topped by barbed wire, with security guards and attack dogs guarding the electric gates at the front of their homes. Thus, there is an all-pervading sense of personal insecurity that haunts South Africa's population, in a way that, for example, is not present in Israel, though Israel's diplomatic and political situation is far more volatile than South Africa's. And there is very little faith or confidence in the police and legal authorities. It has been established and widely publicized that the judicial and police authorities have been irredeemably corrupted by the tribal gangs, organized crime, and even small-time petty criminals. Because of this, armed-response private security services abound, and the security business is certainly one of the major growth industries in South Africa.

The government's attitude towards this problem is apparently one of some ambivalence. On one hand, Mandela has expressed himself as seeing the crime epidemic in South

Africa as being merely one of the "growing pains" in a society transmuting itself from dictatorial, police-state rule to a democratic, less disciplined, and more open form of society. On the other hand, the government is well aware of the continuing steady flight of whites from South Africa, a flight that is clearly linked to the wave of violent crime and fear generated by the transition from apartheid to a more democratic system of communal life.

The Jewish community is racked with a profound sense of angst regarding its future in South Africa. Its population has shrunk by a third over the past decades, and the rate of Jewish emigration from South Africa is now high and apparently rising. This is especially true for the young adults, and the Jewish community there is undergoing a demographic shift and becoming a rapidly aging group that needs more health/retirement facilities than it needs more schools. None of this bodes well for the future of the South African Jewish community.

However, there are enormous bright lights that illuminate the story of South African Jewry. Over the past decade many, many hundreds of previously nonobservant and somewhat alienated Jewish families have become *baalei teshuvah* and have created a strong, dynamic, youthful. and enthusiastic Orthodox Jewish community. This has been true mainly in the city of Johannesburg, but there has also been a significant strengthening of Jewish life in Capetown over the past few years. All of this is due to the appearance and efforts of a number of wonderfully talented rabbinic couples on the South African scene. Ohr Samayach Institutions in Johannesburg has spearheaded this movement of spiritual return, and they have had serious help from other organizations, such as Chabad, which operates a large and successful Jewish educational system for children and adults, the Johannesburg Kollel, and other devoted individuals, both lay and rabbinic. There is an intensive community-wide program of education and social bonding that precedes all Jewish marriages intended to be solemnized by an Orthodox rabbi in South Africa. For many young couples this is their first serious exposure to Jewish knowledge and values, and this program has proven enormously successful in attracting new Jewish couples to an observant, Torah-centered way of life. A number of devoted and talented women have trained tens of other young women to be instructors in this program, thereby compounding its reach and effectiveness both in Johannesburg and in Capetown. New synagogues have sprouted to service young adult couples and even singles. Yeshivos have been established in Capetown and Johannesburg, and there is a great deal of quality Jewish education taking place in South Africa.

There are many reasons for the appearance and strength of the *baal teshuvah* movement in South Africa. South African Jewry has always been traditional, if not particularly knowledgeable or observant. Most South African Jews attend an Orthodox synagogue on Friday nights and then celebrate a Friday night/Sabbath family dinner, even though most of them are not really Sabbath observant in the halachic sense. The standards of *kashrus* supervision are high, and there is no taint of monetary corruption present. Kosher products are widely available, and the seal of the Beth Din of Johannesburg is prominently displayed on scores of manufactured food products available at stores throughout the country.

The South African Jewish community is basically heterogeneous in nature and origin. Over 85 percent of South African Jews are descendants of *litvaks* — Lithuanian Jews — who arrived in South Africa at the end of the 19th century and the beginning of the 20th century. Thus, a great deal of the divisiveness and cultural clashing that characterize less homogeneous Jewish societies, such as those in the United States and Israel, is absent on the South African Jewish scene. The idyllic weather conditions, the natural beauty of the country, the courteous, "laid-back" attitude and life-style of South African society, all contribute to an atmosphere that allows time for contemplation and self-discovery. And a wonderful group of young South African Jews, themselves *baalei teshuvah* and educated at Ohr Somayach College in Jerusalem, returned to South Africa and constructed a magnificent infrastructure of traditional Judaism that has attracted and influenced thousands of their fellow Jewish compatriots. Thus, in the midst of the painful transitions and unclear future of South African life, the Jewish community there is in the midst of reconstructing itself in a positive, traditional, Torah-oriented direction.

A visit to the game reserve at Kruger National Park is a memorable, lifelong, and wondrous experience. The animals are in their natural habitat, ignoring the puny humans driving on the marked roads and trails through the park, bent on achieving photographic immortality. The grace of the loping giraffe, the majesty of the lolling male lion observing the other lions in his pride in the late-afternoon sun, the enormous bulk of six- and seven-ton elephants eating entire trees near the motor trail, the brazenness of the hyenas openly patrolling the motor trails and roads, all contribute to a feeling of wonderment and near-awe. This is what the world must have looked and felt like at the beginning of time! The ant heaps and termite heaps, which take centuries to construct, as every ant and termite contributes one grain of earth, become mounds many feet tall and wide, and are literally castles of wonder. The elegance, symmetry, and ferociousness of nature are all on display in abundance at Kruger National Park. I am told by those who have visited the game reserves of Kenya and Tanzania that they are impressive beyond description; however, South Africa's Kruger National Park certainly has nothing to be ashamed of.

The city of Capetown is probably the single most beautiful city in the world. It is nestled among breathtaking mountain views, surrounded by two oceans, and blessed with peaceful bays that are stopovers for migrating whales. The problem of crime, so overriding in Johannesburg, is more subliminal in Capetown. There has therefore been a steady migration of people from Johannesburg to Capetown, but the major outflow of people from Johannesburg is directed out of the country and not to other cities in South Africa. The Jewish community of Capetown, like that of Johannesburg, is experiencing a renaissance, albeit on a somewhat smaller scale. The sheer physical beauty of Capetown and its civilized quality of life make it a truly rare urban center in this world. The devoted efforts of an American rabbinic couple and the presence of a yeshivah Beis Medrash, staffed by rotating cadres of Israeli yeshivah students, has made a strong impression upon a previously lackadaisical Jewish community. The strength and eternal vitality of Torah and Jewish spiritual life is proven once more by the revival of the Jewish community of Capetown and of South Africa generally. It is this realization that proved most heartening to me in my assessment of the South African visit.

Whenever and wherever I travel to visit Jewish communities throughout the world, I am always impressed by the inherent unity that Torah has created amongst Jews who otherwise share different citizenship, cultures, and life-styles. The words of Saadia Gaon of ninth-century Babylonia ring true more than a millennium later: "Our nation is a nation only because of its Torah." All of our leaders who speak of unity and continuity in Jewish life would do well to remember Saadia's insightful words. There is no other balm for our wounds except Torah, its study, its observance, its support, its centrality in our personal and communal lives. If one needs any empiric proof of this simple fact, let him visit South Africa and its Jewish community.

America the Beautiful

Before embarking on our life-changing move to Jerusalem in July 1997, my wife and I spent two weeks visiting the American Southwest, specifically Arizona and Utah. Whenever I have been able to visit places of great natural beauty, I have always sensed a connection to the process of creation and hence to the Creator. Thus, this has been my experience at all of the beautiful and breathtaking spots on this earth that I have visited: Yosemite, Yellowstone, Banff, Alaska, Capetown, Kruger, Provence, the Alps, and the Dead Sea. But even after seeing all of those places of enchantment and wonderment, I was unprepared for the emotional involvement with creation that the national and state parks of Arizona and Utah engender. In America, the beautiful can truly be seen as the handiwork of G–d the Creator. So, even though descriptions of summer vacations, like home videos of family barbecues, can be boring to uninvolved, innocent third parties, even lethally so, I nevertheless wish to share with you my experiences in Arizona and Utah this past July.

We arrived in Phoenix late at night, but the heat of the desert day still hung in the air. Daytime temperatures in the range of 100-110 degrees Fahrenheit are the norm throughout the summer months. North of Phoenix, on the way to the Grand Canyon National Park, is the community of Sedona. The rock formations and surrounding scenery are magnificently artistic in design and color. A jeep tour into the middle of the rocky forest to witness the sunset colors reflected on the tall surrounding cliffs is a balm to the soul. In Sedona, there is a prominent sign on a large empty lot that states: "Here will rise the Jewish Community Center of Sedona." As a further indication of the presence of some Jewish life in Sedona, there is a large sign in the main supermarket indicating the kosher meat section, though our search through the store revealed no such product available at the time.

The beauty and majesty of Sedona, however, are minor league in comparison to its northern neighbor, Grand Canyon National Park. Since a description of the Grand Canyon of the Colorado River is impossible with words, and even with camera, I will restrict myself to sharing with you my emotions standing there at the South Rim of the canyon. The vastness of the scene, the unbelievable colors, the staggering depth of the canyon are all drowned out in the overwhelming silence of the place. Rarely before have I experienced such a deep, penetrating, almost frightening stillness. Paradoxically, one can almost *hear* that silence, so all-enveloping is it. Standing there, overlooking Creation itself, I thought to myself, "How noisy our world has become!" The rabbis and prophets of Israel described G–d as being heard, so to speak, in haunting, fragile, shattering silence. Well, G–d's silence still pervades the Grand Canyon. And it is that silence, even more than the magnificence of the sight, that overawes one. I feel that this awe is the sensation that Adam must have felt being ushered into a world of such complex splendors, dangers, and beauty. It is as though the entire world itself, in its raw and overwhelming beauty, is that Garden of Eden where human civilization began. How fortunate we are to have a piece of that heavenly garden preserved for viewing, enjoyment, and contemplation.

Though it is only 27 miles across the Grand Canyon as the proverbial crow flies, it is a drive of 162 miles by state roads from the South Rim to the North Rim observation point of the Canyon. The view from the North Rim is different, naturally, than from the South Rim, but the silence and feeling of the place is the same. The July weather at the Canyon is hot during the day and bearably pleasant after dark. The lodgings are adequate but not luxurious. The experience of the Grand Canyon is indelible.

But as grand as the Grand Canyon is, there are national parks in Utah that rival it for overall beauty and wonderment, though each place has its own imprint and character. One of the amazing qualities of nature is that there are really no two things exactly alike. Man may desire to clone himself, but nature does not. Thus, even though the Colorado River and its tributaries, such as the Little Colorado and the Virgin Rivers, are the main catalysts for all the rock and canyon formations that dominate this landscape, they chose not to form each canyon or cliff in a like fashion. Hence, the unending variety and constant surprises of joyful viewing that Arizona and Utah offer to the visitor.

Zion National Park is an Eden of its own. Its rock formations and colors bedazzle and literally entertain you. It also mocks your word processor and camera, for only being there can capture its aura, majesty, serenity, and symmetry. I was told that the park rangers at Zion never apply for early retirement but rather attempt to prolong their tour of duty at all costs. When you are in the park, it is hard to imagine anyone wanting to leave its confines, so great is the hold of its beauty upon you, visually and emotionally. No wonder that the early Mormon explorers who first stumbled into this place of natural wonderment called it Zion.

Near Zion is Bryce National Park, home of amphitheaters of stone which house magnificently yet weirdly shaped rock statues rising hundreds of feet from the floor of the canyon. The rains, the river, the wind, and the interaction among all of the forces of nature have formed these "hoodoos," as they are called. Viewing the "hoodoos" affords one participation in the ultimate Rorschach test, for one's imagination and the endless variety of configurations of these "hoodoos" allows him to see whatever he wishes in those stone monuments of the world's natural history. It is possible for the strong and hearty to hike down to the base of these "hoodoos" and view them from the bottom up, since all of the standard viewing points in Bryce are at the top. Just as in all matters of life, these two types of views give one quite different perspectives on the same object of observation and discussion.

The Glen Canyon Dam project is the most controversial one in the history of the dam projects of the Department of the Interior. Congress approved the construction of the dam during the Eisenhower administration, and the completion of the dam created the second largest man-made lake (the largest is in Egypt behind the Aswan Dam) in the world, Lake Powell. The environmental lobby has been trying to undo the dam since its construction, while the power and urban interests (Phoenix lives because of the water and the electric power from the Glen Canyon Dam on the Colorado River) loudly proclaim its benefits to the development of the economy of the American Southwest. It is unlikely that the dam will disappear in the foreseeable future, no matter how conservationist-minded America may become, and Lake Powell has for now become a tourist attraction of large dimensions. A four-hour round trip by boat on Lake Powell will allow one to view one of the natural wonders of the world — the great Rainbow Natural Bridge — a stone arch of luminous shades of beige and brown of such immense size that under its towering roof five Empire State Buildings, stacked one on top of another, can easily fit.

From Lake Powell, we traveled north into Utah and spent time in Moab, the gateway to Arches National Park. On the way one drives through Monument Valley, whose rocks, cliffs, buttes, and canyons provide stereotypical backdrops of the old West that we carry in our imaginations. As I drove through the area, I kept a wary eye out for the Indian raiding parties that were undoubtedly observing me as I drove through their lands. It is a place of rugged grandeur and serves as a proper introduction to the other-worldly landscape of Arches National Park.

In Arches there are well over 100 natural arches of stone, many of them weirdly and precariously balanced. There are also wondrous rock formations. It is truly a wonderland, and there are parts of the park that give one the impression that he is on another planet. I was looking for the Mars robot Land-rover to appear at many places that I visited! Arches seems like a natural theme park that entices visitors to come and view its wonders. The arches change form as one views them from different directions on the road, and it is impossible not to be emotionally moved by the wildness and strange beauty of the place.

Next to Arches National Park there is another great park called Canyonlands National Park. As the name implies, the park, which is enormous in size and accessible mainly by foot or horse, is a place of beautiful canyons carved by the Colorado River and its tributaries. After seeing the Grand Canyon it is hard to be impressed by any lesser canyons, no matter how numerous and beautiful; nevertheless, Canyonlands is an inspiring place and a worthy addition to and competitor of these other outstanding places of natural wonder in the American Southwest. Why Arizona and Utah should possess so many places of beauty in such concentration and within a relatively small geographic area, while other areas of the United States are relatively barren, demands a congressional investigation. The wonders of these two states are almost too much to bear, absorb, and appreciate in one visit. They demand subsequent visits and time to contemplate and absorb the sights.

My wife and I spent the last Shabbos of our trip in Park City, Utah. This was an old mining town that died in the 1960s and rose again in the 1970s and 1980s as a luxury ski resort town. Shopping in the large local supermarket on Friday afternoon, we discovered a wide variety of kosher foods, even complete glatt kosher prepared meals. We also met a delightful woman from London, England, in the aisle fronting the kosher food section, who told us that there is a nucleus of a Jewish community forming in Park City. There is a very small Jewish presence in

Utah, even in Salt Lake City; there are less than two million inhabitants in Utah and 77% of them are Mormons. Nevertheless, as almost everywhere in the world, there are Jews, and many of them are struggling mightily to remain so.

There is a verse in Psalms which sums up the basic human, and certainly Jewish, emotion that all visits and vacations to places of great natural beauty invoke: "Who can express the awesome quality of G–d's works? Who can make others hear all of the necessary praises for His wonders?" There is a blessing in Jewish tradition that one recites every spring when he first views the newly blossoming fruit trees in their riotously colorful garb: "Blessed are You, O L–rd our G–d, King of the universe, Who has not left anything wanting in His universe, and has created therein good and great creatures, as well as goodly trees, so that man would derive pleasure therefrom." May I be so bold as to paraphrase the words of the great Rabbis of Israel who composed this beautiful blessing and say: Blessed is the G–d of the universe, Who has allowed man to view such wonders as the Grand Canyon of the Colorado River and all of its adjacent parks and reserves, so that man may derive pleasure, inspiration, serenity, and a sense of immortal time and eternal silence therefrom.

The Arizona Memorial

The eight islands which comprise the State of Hawaii are undoubtedly some of the most beautiful locations on G–d's earth. The sea in all of its gentility and fury, mountains and still active volcanoes, lush green valleys with waterfalls and permanent rainbows, exotic flowers, birds, and fish, warm winds and shining sun, all combine to make this place in the middle of the Pacific Ocean, 2,500 miles away from any other land, a veritable paradise.

Yet this is also a place of bitter memories and tragic history. The U.S. Navy base at Pearl Harbor on the island of Oahu was the scene of terrible destruction on the morning of December 7, 1941. In less than two hours on that fateful Sunday morning, the carrier-based planes of the Japanese Imperial Navy destroyed most of the fighting vessels of the United States Pacific Fleet and almost all the planes of the United States Air Force stationed in Hawaii. Eleven American battleships were hit and put out of action. Nine of them were eventually raised from their watery graves, repaired and refurbished, and sent out to take vengeance against the Japanese. Two of the battleships, Utah and Arizona, were never salvaged and still lie on the sandy bottom of the lagoon at Pearl Harbor. Arizona sank in less than 15 minutes after an armor-piercing bomb tore through its deck and exploded in the ammunition/gunpowder storage chamber, and 1,177 American sailors are still entombed in the wreck of that great dreadnought. In commemoration of them and of that dark day in American history, the National Parks Service built and maintains the Arizona Memorial, located in the middle of the lagoon at Pearl Harbor, directly straddling the underwater hulk of that ill-fated ship.

My wife and I were fortunate to spend a few days in Hawaii one winter. One of the sights that we visited was the Arizona Memorial. There was a time when the wait in line to view the memorial stretched to four hours. Today, over 50 years after the event, the wait is down to 40 minutes. Most of the visitors are Japanese. The memorial is extremely moving, especially to someone like me who vividly remembers December 7, 1941 — "a date that will live in infamy." Under the floating memorial lies Arizona with its dead, decaying and forming a new coral reef in this subtropical lagoon. The outline of the ship and its mighty but useless guns can clearly be seen through the clear turquoise waters of the lagoon. The top of one gun turret still rises mournfully out of the water. In the hall of the memorial is a large marble wall upon which are engraved the names of the 1,177 young Americans who died with Arizona that day. And all around is the soothing roll of the sea as it enters the lagoon, the gorgeous mountains of Oahu in the background, everything bathed in the warm winter sun of renewal. How could such a paradise have been turned into such devastation? How cruel and shortsighted of man to have perpetrated this folly!

I wonder about the thoughts and emotions of the Japanese tourists, many of them in their 60s and 70s, as they view this place. They, more than anyone, should realize the terrible futility of that day of their national triumph. Millions would die in the struggle to avenge Arizona. As Arizona lies at rest under its memorial, it mutely testifies to unlimited human cruelty and miscalculation. "Not by might nor by force, but by My spirit alone, says the L–rd of Hosts." That is the true meaning, the lasting emotion, of the ever haunting Arizona Memorial.

VI
NATURE

Trees

In November 1995 there were two major windstorms that
struck Monsey, the community where my wife and I then
resided. The first storm uprooted a tall maple tree that had
been a reassuring fixture on our front lawn. In fact, it preceded the building of our house on this piece of land 30
years ago. Two weeks later another major windstorm struck our
front lawn, felling a tall spruce tree that had been the companion
of the maple for so many years. Our lawn now looked desolate
and bare to me. Every morning as I left my home, I felt deprived
and lonely seeing the emptiness of the lawn in front of me with
only the up-ended root systems of the departed trees showing
through the earth, marking the spots where those majestic trees
had ruled. I was surprised at my reaction to the loss of these two
trees since I had hardly paid them notice while they stood sentry
over my house for decades. Their disappearance caused me to
think about trees, a subject which was not at the forefront of my
"thinking" agenda before the windstorm occurred.

Joyce Kilmer, the famed British poet who was killed in action
in World War I, wrote that "poems are made by fools like me,

but only G–d can make a tree." The connection of trees, perhaps more than any other form of nature, to the Creator is readily apparent in the Torah and Talmud. Eternal life and knowledge are represented in the Garden of Eden in the form of trees. The wanton destruction of trees by man is expressly forbidden by Jewish law. In fact, the human race itself is described in the Torah as being a tree: "For man is as the tree of the field." All later Jewish thought and practice has been influenced by the use of trees as the metaphor for human life in the Bible and the Talmud. Trees, therefore, like all other life phenomena, bear study and contemplation, for they can aid us in our never-ending search for ourselves and our destiny. So here are a few thoughts of mine about trees and their lessons for us humans.

A number of years ago my wife and I were able to spend a few days in Yosemite National Park. Among the awesome wonders of nature that can be viewed there is a famous grove of sequoia trees. They are the oldest living things on our planet, some of them already thousands of years old. They are massive in height and girth. If one needs a lesson in humility, in appreciating our truly diminutive status in the natural world, standing in the midst of that grove of sequoia trees in Yosemite will do nicely. As the park ranger explained their growth and existence and as the immensity of the trees gradually overwhelmed us, a tremendous hush, a palpable silence, filled the air of the grove. I thought to myself then, "I am standing next to a living creation of G–d that was living when the Temple in Jerusalem still stood on its foundation, when Rome was the colossus of the world, and there was no London, Paris, or New York. What wonderful secrets it could tell if it could only speak!" And then I realized that it was sharing with me a great secret about life merely by its presence — the secret of patience, of time, of being unhurried.

The park ranger pointed to a small bushlike tree that was about 40 inches tall, situated about 30 yards away from the grove of the great sequoias. "What species of tree is that?" he asked the assembled visitors. None of us amateur botanists answered. "Why, that is a sequoia tree," he answered. Sensing our amazement, he added, "It is only about 80 years old. Give it time, and it will also be hundreds of feet tall like its brother sequoias over here."

Ah, time, that most precious of all commodities, fleeting, irreplaceable, and often abused. Humans are not blessed with the life span of the sequoia. The Psalms teach us that the years of our lives are "70, or by dint of courageous strength, 80." Modern medicine and technology can stretch those limits, but not by much. So our nature is to be in a great hurry, impatient, realizing that our clock is constantly ticking. We want instant answers, instant gratification, instant results, because we know that there is not much time left for us. Yet it is patience, the ability to allow time to work its magic, its healing, that truly encourages and defines human progress. The question the sequoia poses to us is: "What will our world and our efforts therein look like one, or two, or five centuries from now?" The G-d of history has infinite patience to wait for the reply. We can only imitate Him in attempting to achieve the blessing of some sense of patience in our personal, hurried lives.

In the *Ethics of the Fathers* we are taught that there are two types of trees, representative of two types of humans. There are trees that may grow very tall and give the appearance of eternal mightiness, but which have a very shallow root system. These trees are subject to destruction in a major windstorm. Their very height and might allows the wind to topple them, and their shallow roots do not have the depth and leverage to hold them erect in the fierce winds. However, there are other trees that have very strong and developed root structures, with the roots finding their way deep into the ground. Such a tree will ride out the storm and resist being uprooted and broken by the force of the strong winds that attack it.

So too, the Rabbis taught us, is it with human beings. Someone who is deeply rooted in faith, in the traditions and values that have defined civilization since Sinai, will be able to withstand all of the hostile storms that challenge all good people in their lives. The strengths of family and of home, of secure and positive relationships, of godly values untainted by human corruption and cynicism, are all means for planting our roots deep into the ground. If, in the words of the Rabbis, "one's fear of sin and heaven is paramount over his concept of personal wisdom," then there are no winds that can upset his balance and destroy his tree of life. However, if "one's sense of personal wisdom is paramount over any concept of fear of sin or heaven," as is unfortunately true in much of the modern world, then the tree of life is perched very precariously and is liable to be completely uprooted by a forceful wind, no matter how temporary the storm. Trees therefore teach us most vividly the importance of deep root structures in our lives. The stumps of the two trees on my front lawn, torn from the earth by the violent wind that ended their lives, give mute evidence daily as to the inadequateness of their shallow root structures. As I gazed upon them every morning when leaving my home, the lesson of deep roots was reinforced within me.

When I lived in Miami Beach over 25 years ago, my family and I had the dubious honor of experiencing a number of direct hits on our home from hurricanes. The almost human shriek of winds in excess of 125 miles per hour pierced my innermost soul. I was convinced that none of the trees that flanked our street or were planted in our front lawn or backyard would survive that onslaught. Yet, on the morning after the hurricane, when we were free to venture forth outside the house, I was astounded to see that all of the trees had survived, though some had lost foliage. A number of streets away, however, all of the large, majestic, imposing royal palms were leveled. It was the ability of the more flexible, less rigid coconut palms to bow before the wind that enabled them to survive the hurricane.

The great and haughty royal palms that grow straight to the sky are wonderful for fine weather. They don't stand much chance of survival in a hurricane. The Talmud uses that exact metaphor in explaining Israel's unique ability to survive in an often very hostile world. "It is the bullrushes that bend their head in the wind that survive, not the tall and mighty trees that refuse to humble themselves and are therefore uprooted." The art of survival is not glamorous or especially heroic. But the Jewish people learned a long time ago that the art of survival requires a low profile, the ability to remain hidden and silent, and a flexibility of tactics (not beliefs), combined with a sense of patience to ride out the storm. Rigid behavior and outmoded tactics spell certain defeat in life. Just look at the trees in the midst of a windstorm and you will see what I mean.

Quite a number of years ago, the remnants of a southern hurricane traveling up the eastern coast of the United States inflicted severe damage in the area where I resided. Two large trees in my backyard were broken off at their trunks, one of which unfortunately fell on my neighbor's house, causing some damage. The tree surgeons arrived to remove the trees and in that process sawed the trees down nearly to the base of their trunks. However, the root systems of both trees were apparently unaffected. Soon, new branches began to grow out of the sides of those shortened trunks. Those branches have grown tall and healthy over the years, so that in spring and summer the trees are clothed in verdant beauty and provide blessed shade. Unless one looks very closely, one cannot tell that these trees have shortened trunks and once were really "dead," at least in the landscaper's definition of that dreaded word. Yet here they are, beautiful, alive, and fresh as ever, due to the life force of their root systems and the amazing, divine power of regeneration which the Creator has infused into all of His living creatures.

To me these trees symbolize the recuperative power of humans in the face of all adversities. The unconquerable spirit of humans is the highest reflection of the godly soul within us. The Jewish response to tragedy, both personal and national, has been to go on and rebuild and regenerate and reproduce. Is that not really the story of Jewish life in our century? The handful of great men and women who rebuilt the Torah world over the past 50 years were, in the main, Holocaust survivors. The State of Israel is a product of Jewish regenerative tenacity after the horrors of World War II. If the roots are there, the tree will yet give forth new branches and leaves. Maimonides, in a letter to one of his students who was apparently depressed about the situation of 12th-century Jewry, proposed the following metaphor: In the autumn when leaves begin to fall from the tree, every leaf that falls from the tree says, "Woe to the poor tree which will be left so barren and empty without me." But in reality, the leaf should weep for itself and not for its host tree. For when the depressing and cold winter ends and the warm spring sun returns, the tree will put forth new leaves and cover itself in beauty once more. But the poor leaf is dead forever, for its vitality was solely dependent upon its attachment to the tree.

So too is it with Jews and the tree of life — the tree of Torah and tradition, of moral values and holy life. Many Jews who drift away from their heritage, who remove their leaf from the tree of Jewish experience, nevertheless feel nostalgic and sorry for the tree — "How will it survive the winter when all of its leaves have deserted it?" The truth of the matter is that the Jewish people and its Torah is eternal — they are the tree of life itself. Our task is to see that somehow, at all costs, our leaf remains attached to that tree. That is the true meaning of the Biblical verse that states that the Torah "is the tree of life to all those who uphold it, who cling to it." Perhaps next time you notice a tree you will think of the great spiritual lesson that it represents and appreciate both the spiritual and physical beauty of a tree — this marvelous creation of the G–d of the universe.

Silence Is...

Many years ago my wife and I spent a peaceful and holy Sabbath at Kibbutz Lavie, near the Horns of Hittin, 18 kilometers southwest of Lake Kineret in the Land of Israel. We went for a Sabbath eve stroll under the stars of the Lower Galilee, and I remember that while walking I was disturbed by something indefinable and troublesome. Not until we finally returned to the guest house of the kibbutz to retire for the night did I hone in on the source of my gnawing discontent. It was the silence, the frightening, awe-inspiring, deafening, all-pervasive silence of the night that discomforted me. No motors, no traffic or airplanes, no radios, televisions, shouts, or even animal, bird, or insect noises were to be heard — only the stillness of the silent Sabbath evening. It frightened me. I was out of my milieu, ripped from my world of constant sound, of background music and conversation, of the roar of the not-too-distant highway and the ring of the ubiquitous telephone, and all of the other raucous noises of modern civilization. The silence gave me the creeps. I shivered, though the night was pleasantly warm. Since that Galilean night 26 years ago, I have rarely thought about that frightening experience of silence, not wanting to explore it too deeply, afraid of what I would discover about myself if I pursued it. So I drowned that experience of silence in the ocean of sound that continually surrounds me.

A number of months ago I was flying from Chicago, my old home, to Monsey, with the plane due to land at Newark Airport. It was a day of fierce winds aloft and on the ground, and the plane bumped along erratically. On such flights, the plane becomes a very still place. The foolhardiness of being 30,000 feet in the air in such a heavy machine, defying all laws of gravity and common sense and relying for safety and life itself upon certain principles of physics not clearly understood by most people, is then apparent to all of the passengers strapped into their seats. I attempted to divert myself by glancing at the airline company's magazine in the seat pocket in front of me.

There was an article in that issue written by a California public-relations executive about his search for peace, solitude, and rest. He wrote of checking himself into a monastery in the California desert for a weekend. The monastery, suffering from low occupancy and dwindling income, has turned itself into an inn, renting rooms to jaded Los Angelinos searching for — something. Business at the monastery has been brisk, with all of its rooms regularly booked on weekends and most of them occupied even in midweek. The food at the monastery is simple and bland and does not cry out for seconds. The rooms are simply and sparsely furnished and are bereft of telephones, faxes, televisions, radios, stereos, and all other necessary accouterments of modern life. The author found all of the above intriguing, perhaps even comforting. But what ruined his weekend at the monastery was the nightly imposition of The Great Silence. The monastic rules forbid any conversation from 8:30 p.m. until after breakfast of the next morning. Guests also have to abide by The Great Silence. Talk about torture!

The Great Silence forced the guest to face himself, his life, his problems, his shortcomings. Instead of the silence giving him comfort and serenity, it stirred him into turmoil.

Initially, he was disturbed instead of calmed, fearful instead of assured, empty instead of fulfilled. But by the time the weekend at the monastery ended, he felt more knowing about himself, more humble and sensitive, and less driven and aggressive. He saw life and himself in a different perspective. He reserved a room for himself at the monastery for six months later, knowing that by then he would need The Great Silence again in order to refresh his true, inner, soulful self.

Lo and behold, as I finished reading the article I noticed that the plane had safely landed and we were at the gate ready to deplane. The noise of the engines, the passengers, and the general tumult of the airport now sounded deafening in my ears. For the first time in a long time, I too thought about silence and its benefits.

The Torah teaches us that G–d is not clearly heard or discerned in the great noisy rush of the wind, or in the incessant cackle of the fire, or through the shouts of victors and vanquished. Rather, He is heard only in the still, small voice, in the silence of prayer sincerely expressed, in the quiet human acceptance of sadness, mortality, and even tragedy. That is why the Torah places such an emphasis on holy speech and its equally holy companion, silence. The Talmud states: "A word is worth a golden coin. Silence is worth two such coins." A synagogue should be a place of silence, not of noise. A home, a family, a marriage, is built upon the blessing of sensitive moments of silence. One rarely regrets what one did not say. This blessing of studied silence allows for contemplation, growth, security, and eventual inner peace. Silence is more than golden. It exposes us to the essence of spirituality, and it becomes the guardian of godly behavior in man.

In Search of the Elusive Chilazon

When I was in Chicago last September, I had the honor of addressing the student body of my alma mater yeshivah, Hebrew Theological College. After my address, one of the younger *roshei yeshivah*, Rabbi E. Twerski, thrust into my hand an unpublished article of his regarding the *chilazon*, a lizard/snail-like creature from whose blood a bluish-purple dye was manufactured. This dye was used to manufacture the *techeiles* string that the Torah mentions in regard to the commandment of *tzitzis*, the stringed fringes required on four-cornered garments worn by Jews. The manufacture of this rare dye disappeared in Jewish society in the early seventh century. Thus, for almost 1200 years, no *techeiles* existed amongst Jews, and even stranger is the fact that until the late 19th century, no attempt was made to reintroduce its production.

However, for the past century, a fantastic Talmudic halachic detective story has taken place in the Jewish world. A determined effort has been mounted to rediscover the *chilazon* so that the *techeiles* dye can again be available and the Biblical commandment of *tzitzis* fulfilled in its truest form. As can be imagined, in a reconstructive project of this nature and magnitude, different solutions to the problem of identifying the true *chilazon* have been proposed, attacked, and vehemently defended. Rabbi Twerski's article deals with this fascinating story of the search for the *chilazon*. I am herewith unashamedly summarizing that article for the benefit of the readers of this book.

One of the great chassidic leaders of the past century was Rabbi Gershon Henoch Leiner, the Radziner Rebbe. A scholar and a creative genius, he was a controversial figure in the chassidic world because of certain of his innovations and writings. In 1887, he published a work maintaining that the *chilazon* was not extinct and that there was no practical or halachic reason that *tzitzis* containing a *techeiles* string could be manufactured and worn by Jews. However, the *chilazon* had to be identified. Rabbi Leiner addressed himself to this task, traveling to Italy to visit aquariums containing Mediterranean sea-life. After much research and observation, Rabbi Leiner proclaimed that the *chilazon* was a species of cuttlefish called *sepia officinalis*. Using the blood of this fish, Rabbi Leiner attempted to produce *techeiles*. However, he encountered many difficulties in transferring his theory into practice, chiefly because the blood of that cuttlefish was black in color, while the *techeiles* was always presumed to be blue or perhaps purple in color. Let us therefore leave Rabbi Leiner in the middle of his *techeiles* experiment and discuss the color itself.

There are currently two main theories as to the true color of *techeiles*. One is that *techeiles* is a shade of purple bordering on a royal blue. This is the view of Dr. I. Ziederman, published in the scholarly journal *Techumim*, Volume 9. His reasoning rests upon the Talmudic statement that there always existed a group of fraudulent *techeiles* merchants who manufactured their product not from the dye base of the blood of the *chilazon*, but rather from *k'la ilan*, a vegetable dye that produced a color exactly like it. In order to differentiate between the real and the ersatz, the Talmud describes a method of chemical testing. The chemicals will fade *k'la ilan*, but will not affect true *techeiles*. If the dye obtained from the *chilazon* is indigo blue, Dr. Ziederman maintains that it too will fade, for that one-color component dye is subject to the same chemical effects as *k'la ilan*. However, if the color of *techeiles* is purple, then the ersatz dye had to be made from a combination of indigo and red. It is this red dye component that will be affected by the chemicals, and that is why the pure *techeiles* will not fade, while *k'la ilan* will fade.

The vast majority of scholars disagree with the purple-color theory of Dr. Ziederman and are of the opinion that the true color of *techeiles* is indigo-blue. This is based on the Talmudic statement that *techeiles* is the color of the sea and the sky, neither of which are normally purple. Traditionally, the Jewish people always thought of *techeiles* as being blue, and the Greeks, in their writings about the Jews, referred to *techeiles* as being "hyacinth," which in the ancient world was always a blue flower. Various explanations have been advanced for how the chemical test proposed by the Talmud would operate on a blue dye, though, none of them, if the truth be said, are completely satisfying. Yet most scholars are convinced that the direct evidence in favor of blue as being the color of *techeiles* far outweighs the indirect evidence of Dr. Ziederman that the color is somehow purple. In any event, it is clear that *techeiles* cannot be manufactured from a black dye, and the blood of the cuttlefish is black. So let us now return to Rabbi Leiner and his experiment.

Rabbi Leiner enlisted the aid of a chemist to determine how the original black blood of the cuttlefish could be made into a blue dye. The chemist introduced chemical additives to the cuttlefish blood (iron, potash, ammonium chloride, muratic acid, sulfuric acid, and tartaric acid) and synthesized the blood into a dye known as Prussian blue. Rabbi Leiner assumed that since all of the chemical additives were colorless, the resultant blue dye was somehow inherent in the black blood of the cuttlefish. Rabbi Leiner made *techeiles* his lifetime project. Thus, many scholars and leading European rabbis, convinced by the weight of his scholarly evidence, his three books on the subject, his holy reputation for piety and spirituality, and the strength and certainty of his conviction, actually agreed to the validity of *sepia officinalis*, the cuttlefish, as the true *chilazon*. The Radziner *chassidim* naturally accepted the opinion of their rebbe, Rabbi Leiner, as fact, and even today Radziner *chassidim* wear *tzitzis* that contain a *techeiles* string made from cuttlefish-blood dye.

Rabbi Isaac HaLevi Herzog, the late chief rabbi of Israel, in a doctoral dissertation submitted in 1913, set out to prove the validity of Rabbi Leiner's theory. However, early in his research, he discovered what many consider to be a fatal flaw in Rabbi Leiner's experiment. His experiments demonstrated that it was not the cuttlefish blood that caused the blue dye, but rather, all of the seemingly colorless chemical additives that had been combined with it. He also determined that organic blood from any creature would, in combination with those chemicals, create Prussian blue dye. According to Rabbi Herzog, Rabbi Leiner had been duped by the chemist upon whom he had relied!

Rabbi Herzog therefore set out on his own to discover the true *chilazon* and the Biblical *techeiles*. His hypothesis was that the *chilazon* was a snail, a shelled creature known as *murex trunculus*. Aside from the chemical evidence that Rabbi Leiner's cuttlefish was not the *chilazon*, Rabbi Herzog had also raised other objections to the cuttlefish. The Talmud tells us that the dye of the *chilazon* was quite expensive, whereas cuttlefish ink is plentiful and cheap. The Talmud also states that the *chilazon* was buried in sand, whereas cuttlefish cannot exist in sand. The *chilazon* is described as having a shell that needed to be cracked in order to extract its blood-dye, and the cuttlefish has no such shell. *Techeles* was described as being a very fast dye, whereas the Prussian blue dye washes out with soap. Rabbi Leiner himself had addressed these objections in his scholarly works defending the cuttlefish as the *chilazon*, but Rabbi Herzog found his arguments forced and his defenses unimpressive. The murex trunculus snail met all of the descriptions of the Talmud, and thus Rabbi Herzog's thesis seemed correct. However, Rabbi Herzog himself hedged on the matter, due to four problems that he himself raised.

His doubts were as follows: The dye of the blood of the *murex trunculus* is really purple and not blue; the dye appears not to be essentially fast or permanent; the body of the murex does not resemble the color of the sea, a requirement described in the Talmud; and the Talmud stated that the *chilazon* appeared only once in 70 years, while the *murex trunculus* is not noted for rare, cyclical appearances on the Mediterranean coast. Rabbi Herzog therefore suggested that perhaps the *chilazon* is actually a snail identified as *janthina*, which meets many, but again not all, of the descriptive criteria of the Talmud.

In recent times new discoveries, both archaeological and technological, have arisen which seem to substantiate Rabbi Herzog's original claim that the *murex trunculus* is the *chilazon*. The basis of Rabbi Herzog's doubts has been removed, or at least mitigated, since scientific experiment has shown that the purple blood of the *murex* turns blue when exposed to sunlight in the process of being converted to a dye. It has also been demonstrated that when this blue dye is properly prepared with the correct reduction agents (those chemicals used to treat the wool so that it will be able to absorb dye), the dye is extremely fast and will not fade or wash out. It is also known now that the *murex* acquires a slimy, sea-colored, algae-type of coating on its shell when it swims in the ocean. Thus, it does resemble the color of the sea, and only when it is washed clean after emerging from the sea does the shell become brown. Many possible answers have been suggested regarding the Talmud's description of the *chilazon* as appearing only once in 70 years, but that question still remains unsolved.

In this century, archaeologists have discovered enormous numbers of broken *murex* shells, buried in large pits near the Phoenician (currently Lebanese) cities of Tyre and Sidon. The Talmud identifies the spawning grounds of the *chilazon* as being located in southern Phoenicia, "from Haifa to Sidon." It has been well established that the centers of the dye industry in the ancient world were Tyre and Sidon. The Talmud explains that the method of extracting blood from the *chilazon* was by cracking open the shell and squeezing the hypobrachial gland. In doing so to a *murex trunculus,* a clear mucus spurts forth. This mucus is originally colorless, but when exposed to the air, it changes from its clear color to yellow, then to green, then to blue, and then to purple. When the blood-dye, now purple, is reduced (deoxidized) in the process of being turned into a dye, and then exposed to direct sunlight, it takes on its permanent blue color. The vast number of broken snail shells found in the Phoenician pits all appear to have been broken open opposite the hypobrachial gland, indicating that they were netted for the purpose of dye-production and not for other purposes, such as food. Thus, there is much circumstantial evidence that supports the idea that the *murex trunculus* is the true, historic *chilazon* of the Bible and the Talmud. Rabbi Herzog's intuition has been proven on target, even though it has not yet been proven beyond doubt.

In Israel today there are a growing number of Jews wearing *techeiles* in their *tzitzis*. Not only the *chassidim* of Radzin, who still adhere to the *techeiles* of Rabbi Gershon Henoch Leiner, but many of the younger generation of Israeli yeshivah students wear *techeiles* daily. The vast majority of *techeiles* manufactured in Israel today comes from the blood-dye of the *murex trunculus*. In any case, the story of the *chilazon* has proven to be fascinating and mysterious. Let us see what will happen with the *chilazon* in the future. This small creature is an integral part of the unfolding story of the Jewish people. Isn't G–d's world spellbinding?

VII

ISRAEL —
THE LAND
AND THE
PEOPLE

Going Home

Jacob flees the wrath of his brother, Esau. He leaves his parents, his home, and his land, and takes up residence with his uncle Laban in Mesopotamia. The round trip of his grandfather Abraham is now apparently complete. The first Jewish family Divinely ordained experiment with the Land of Israel appears to be over. The future of Jacob will be played out in exile, far from the Holy Land. Set first in Mesopotamia and later in Egypt, the story of Jacob is the story of his separation from the homeland promised to him and his descendants by the L–rd of Abraham at the covenantal moment at Mount Moriah. As such, the Torah deals at length with Jacob's struggle to survive and prosper in the hateful and negative environment of Laban's culture. While his aged parents still live in the Land of Israel, it is the presence of Jacob's own twin brother Esau that dominates that country and prevents him from returning home. The Land of Israel is seen by all as being the possession of Esau. His violent sword sits athwart the gates of Zion and Jerusalem. Jacob is doomed to a life of exile.

But Jacob himself never succumbs to the despondency and

bitterness of exile. Even after decades in the house of Laban, he continues to nurture within him and his children the dream of Zion and Jerusalem. Jacob is always "going home." Even in death, he will command his beloved son Joseph to bring him home, to bury him in the ancestral tomb at Machpelah. He is not broken by the discrimination and bigotry he suffers at the hand of his own kinsmen, beneficiaries of his efforts and talents, the family of Laban. Neither will he be dazzled at the end of his life by the tombs of the Pharaohs, the great pyramids and temples of Egyptian society, which are all possibly available to him as well. Better the cave and rocks of Hebron, his home, than the glitter of Aram, Thebes, or Memphis. And this attitude and belief of "going home" became deeply rooted in the lives and psyches of his children and grandchildren as well.

The Jewish people in its long exile always followed this pattern established by their patriarch Jacob. No matter how far away from the Land of Israel we Jews were in terms of time and distance, we were always "going home." It made no difference that only a few old and feeble Jews actually lived in the country and that the swords of Esau and Ishmael alternated in blocking Jewish settlement there Rabbi Yehudah HaLevi summed up the Jewish attitude in his famous poetic line: "My heart is in the East, while I find myself yet in the farthest reaches of the West." It was this ingrained attitude of "going home," of never despairing of the return to our land, that warmed the frost-filled night of the Exile. And somehow in this century a large number of Jews finally made it home.

It is ironic that this achievement has been clouded by a loss of commitment and spirit on the part of many who should know better. Having ignored Jacob and forgotten his teachings and tradition, the sense of "going home" has waned, even amongst those who are physically "home." The current angst of the Jewish people, both in Israel and in the Diaspora, is a crisis of direction and goals. It cannot be eased by governments, agreements, elections, political parties, or national policies. It requires an inner renewal, a spiritual vision, a flight of divinely inspired imagination. It requires that Jacob be part of each of us, part of our hopes and dreams and lives. Then we will always truly be "going home."

Jerusalem 3000 and Rome 2000

I n the next few years those two great cities of Western civilization, continually warred over and contested, Jerusalem and Rome, will mark anniversaries. Much has been made of the 3000th anniversary (give or take a few centuries) of King David's establishment of Jerusalem as the capital of the Jewish state. The municipality of Jerusalem, together with the Israel Ministry of Tourism, implemented a year-long commemoration called "Jerusalem 3000" to celebrate this anniversary. It hoped to attract hundreds of thousands of visitors to see the ancient Holy City in its modern garb, to show them the remaining relics of its past.

But in the typical confusion that marks today's Jewish world and its Jewish state, the type of celebration and the methods of commemoration were hotly debated and contested. Among the events to mark the anniversary were rock concerts, symphonic and operatic performances, stage shows, athletic contests, street fairs, parades, speeches, and a special religious service to be conducted at a large, ornate, and touristy local synagogue. In short, Jerusalem 3000 bore a close resemblance to Bastille Day in France, or the Fourth of July in the United States. I am afraid that not much of King David survived in the celebration of the end of the third millennia of his city. Those who preserve King David in their daily lives — the Jews who recite *Tehillim* (*Psalms*) — were not very well represented amongst the planners of this party, and they were probably just as happy to stay away from the whole event.

Nevertheless, the event and its celebration are important and most instructive. For the commemoration of Jerusalem's 3000th anniversary clearly illustrates the problems that still confront the Holy City and the people of Israel. The hypocritically pious diplomats of the European Community, together with America's Jewish ambassador to Israel, announced boycotts of the event as being too "political," since the true status of Jerusalem is still "undecided and subject to negotiation between the interested parties." The Arab states, even those who have signed peace treaties with Israel, naturally raised a furor over Israel's audacity in sponsoring and publicizing such an event. And the Israeli government itself has lately reversed a decades-long policy of requesting foreign embassies to operate in Jerusalem rather than in Tel Aviv, by publicly lobbying against a bill introduced in the United States Senate authorizing the relocation of the American embassy from Tel Aviv to Jerusalem. The gleeful stock answer that all of the Arabist desk officers at the U.S. State Department now employ when questioned about their obvious pro-Palestinian stance is that they "do not wish to do anything to undermine the Israeli government and its policies." Thus, the Israeli government itself is determined not to take Jerusalem 3000 too seriously. It is, after all, only a publicity stunt, a gimmick to attract more tourists. Not to worry; by 3001, the entire matter will be forgotten.

Yet, as often happens with historical commemorations, the event took on a life of its own, far beyond the schemes and imagination of its planners. Jerusalem 3000 suddenly meant something far more than the publicity gimmick it was originally intended to be. It struck a chord in the deep recesses of the souls of the Jewish masses. It awakened a dormant interest in Jerusalem and King David. It became serious business, not just showy flim flam. It may yet turn out to have been a real and spiritual event, in spite of its banal programing and political embarrassment.

For Jerusalem symbolizes a potent idea — that of the eternity of the people of Israel. The history of the Jewish connection with Jerusalem antedates King David. It was upon Mount Moriah, the Temple Mount of Jerusalem, that Abraham and Isaac entered into the eternal Jewish covenant with the G–d of Israel. It was there that Jacob tarried the night on his way to his exile in the house of Laban. It is the place where the Jews knew their Temple would be built, even though many centuries would elapse between their entry into the Land of Israel and the realization of their dream to construct the house of G–d in the Holy City. Jerusalem came to mean not only a place on the globe, a physical locality, but rather a representation of everything Jewish — the people, the Torah, the Land of Israel, the Messianic Era, the development of human civilization itself. Therefore, when Jews said, "If I forget you, O Jerusalem, let my right hand fail," they stated that Jerusalem encompassed the entire idea of Jewish eternity. The Holy City stood as testimony that there was a holy people, a holy law, a holy purpose in G–d's world.

In faraway medieval Provence, the Jewish street was always named Rue Jerusalem. In Eastern Europe, the great Jewish community in Vilna, renowned for its scholars and intense Jewish life, was known as "Jerusalem of Lithuania." Jews were so Jerusalem-conscious that the non-Jewish world automatically associated the city with the Jews, even though it was a holy city for Christians as well. Mark Twain and the Baedeker's tourist guide (the bible of 19th-century American world tourists) were disappointed by the physical Jerusalem of the late 1880s. But the stalwart Jews of Lithuania, Poland, and Hungary, who emigrated from their birthlands to the Holy City at that very time, were not discouraged or disheartened by the sand, heat, poverty, and privation that Jerusalem exhibited. Rather, in the shimmering sun of the city, these Jews saw Isaiah and David, Hillel and the Maccabees, and were delighted to become their companions in the unfolding of the eternal story of Jerusalem. For to Jews, Jerusalem was always more than a place — it was the Jewish people itself.

Jerusalem today is one of the most beautiful cities on earth. It is a large city with a population nearing 600,000. In spite of terrible traffic problems, suicide bus bombers, and streets whose names change every three blocks, it remains essentially a warm, friendly, lovely, and inspiring place. Its ancient archaeological wonders, splendid and varied museums, and great schools of scholarship exist side by side with outstanding buildings of modern architecture, the most modern and efficient medical centers in the Middle East, enormous indoor shopping malls, and the starkest Biblical landscape and scenic views in the world. And always there is that Jerusalem sun, reflected in the soft golden glow of the stone that covers 98 percent of its buildings. That wonderful sun of heat and light, of blinding intensity and soft shadings, of hope and memory, is the sun that warmed the people of Israel in the coldest climes of the Exile and in the darkest nights of human despair.

And always and everywhere in Jerusalem is the sound of Torah. Scholar and street-sweeper, old and young, Eastern and Western Jews, different in customs and outlook, these Jews of Jerusalem love Torah. They study it, debate it, explore it, write about it, and then debate it again. There are thousands of Jerusalemites engaged exclusively in teaching and studying Torah. It is no wonder that Torah, the people of Israel, and Jerusalem have always been synonymous terms in Jewish life.

But it requires a special view, a Jewish soul — a *Yiddishe neshamah* — to perceive Jerusalem accurately. It is a modest and chaste spot, not given to revealing itself easily. It cloaks itself in the many layers of its mundane urban life, of stadiums and zoos, of commerce and government, of tourism and strangers. As such, there are many who visit the city, or who may even live there, who never see the real Jerusalem. The words of Rabbi Abraham HaCohen of Kalisk, Poland, who settled in Tiberias and visited Jerusalem in 1795, state the truth boldly and beautifully: "Many upsets and tribulations, problems and amazing happenings will occur to every Jew wishing to be part of Jerusalem. The race is not to the swift, and certainly not to the impatient. It is not a matter of a day or two, nor of a month or even a year. But rather, many years must pass before one is absorbed into the life and spirit of the Holy City, this place of refuge under the wing of G–d ... Every Jew is born a Jerusalemite. And thus, when one first comes to Jerusalem, he perforce becomes as an infant once more and must again pass through a childhood and an adolescence, with all of the inherent difficulties that are part of growing up, until he reaches the maturity of seeing the Holy Land and City face to face in its overwhelming spiritual reality, and his soul will become bound to the soul of the Holy Land itself. I have seen pious and great Talmudic scholars arrive here from the Exile, and their initial adjustment is a most difficult and painful one. They lose their stability, their power of analysis, and their talent for creative Torah scholarship. They have no peace, all the imperfections of the land and its people trouble them mightily and give them no ease, they become like a storm-tossed ship floundering in a raging sea. Where is there Torah here? Where are the holy *mitzvos* — the commandments of Sinai? Woe is to me for having left the comfort of my previous home. And then, when all is apparently lost, only then will the countenance of G–d finally shine upon him, and he will at last become serene and comforted. And then he will see the beauty of Jerusalem in all of its glory. There is no timetable or exact schedule for this process, and the length of time it takes will vary from one individual to another. One should therefore steel himself for this reality of Jerusalem and decide if he is up to the challenge. Then he can proceed confidently on the road to Jerusalem."

There is a deep and foreboding feeling in Israel that the government, in spite of its many protestations to the contrary, is prepared to relinquish the current exclusively Jewish control over Jerusalem. For it is obvious from its statements and past behavior that it has never glimpsed the real Jerusalem, and therefore its attitude does not reflect the emotional hold of the city over Jewish history and life. Yoram Hazony, the director of the Shalem Center — National Policy Institute in Jerusalem, in an article that appeared in the October 9, 1995 issue of *The Weekly Standard*, quoted Yoel Marcus, a leading left-leaning columnist for the prestigious Israeli daily newspaper *HaAretz*, as follows: "In their worst nightmares, neither Yitzhak Rabin nor Shimon Peres could have imagined himself 25 years ago as the architect of a government that would take Israel back to its pre-1967 borders. But this is exactly what they are doing ... Leave for a moment the preoccupation with the headlines of the hour [and consider] the really dramatic revolution taking place. Our people have long since tired of bearing Zionism on their shoulders generation after generation. While the Arabs have remained faithful to their ideology of the holiness of the land ... Israel is ready lightly to withdraw from the lands that were the cradle of Judaism [in exchange for] personal safety and a 'normal' life."

Hazony continues: "For 'the handshake,' as the deal with Arafat is known, sought to achieve the heart's desire of 'normal' Israelis by renouncing precisely those emotional assets which allow many 'Jewish' Israelis to lead meaningful lives. And on the heels of this realization has come a second [revelation], the recognition that the Jewish state is sliding headlong into a bitter cultural war. Israel is realigning into two camps: those for whom forgetting about Arafat's murderous past and giving him what he wants mean achieving an exhilarating liberation; and those for whom these concessions mean abandoning the entire purpose of the Jewish state in the first place — a calamity of unfathomable proportions ...

"Israel's schools have been subjected to two decades of progressive dilution of Jewish subjects such as Bible, Talmud, and Jewish history. But the current Labor government outdid its predecessors by installing Shulamit Aloni, of its most radical antireligious fringe, as Minister of Education. In this post, Aloni declared traditional Jewish dietary laws unnecessary, attacking school trips to Auschwitz for stirring up 'nationalist' sentiment among the students, and insisted that references to G–d be eliminated from armed forces memorial services. The educational activities of the deputy minister, Micha Goldman, have included calling for a change in the text of the national anthem, *HaTikvah*, 'in order to give expression to citizens who are not Jews'; advocating that the poetry of Tewfik Ziyad be taught 'next to the poetry' of modern Hebrew bard Chaim Bialik; and ordering a purge of religious teachers in the ministry's school system. The ministry's appointee as chairman of the Committee for History Curriculum Reform is Moshe Zimmerman, who has used the media to compare Orthodox Jewish children to Hitler Youth, the Bible to *Mein Kampf,* and the armed forces to the SS. Says Zimmerman, 'Learning about the Jewish people and the State of Israel appears in the [new educational] program but certainly not as a subject of primary importance.'" Not much room for Jerusalem 3000 here.

Rome 2000, still several years away, also presents a challenge, not only to the Christian world but to the Jewish world as well. The end of the second Christian millennium is a good time for the Church to take stock of itself. It also supplies those outside the Church with their opportunity to rethink their relationship with the Christian religion and more particularly with the Roman Catholic Church, as it is espoused and practiced.

The role of the Church is far different in today's world from what it was for most of the past two millennia of its existence. For its first 1500 years, the Church was an empire and its pope a temporal king. The Church was sovereign over vast territories in Europe, had a large and feared army, persecuted its dissidents and perceived enemies with torture, fury, and barbarity, and attempted to coerce the world into believing in Christian peace by the use of the sword and fiery stake. Such a policy was doomed to failure, which became abundantly apparent only over the last four centuries.

But the Church has now changed and adjusted to meet the times and its new situation. Having no sword and itself under attack from the ravages of secularism, atheism, and divergent views of Christianity, it is now positioning itself as the moral conscience of civilization. It has expanded its missionary activities in Africa and Asia and become the voice of social change and equality in much of Central and South America. But most dramatically, through its pope, the Church is almost the lone major voice speaking out regularly against the cruelty, amorality, licentiousness, and absence of spiritual values in modern society. It is the Church which has taken strong stands against deviant life-styles, the rampant spread of divorce and the destruction of cohesive family units, abortions on demand, euthanasia, and the excesses of the entertainment industry. None of these stands are currently popular or politically correct, certainly not in the secularized Western world. In fact, the public pronouncements of the Church on these issues are not very popular amongst many of its own flock, especially in the English-speaking world in the United States. But the Church has not flinched on these matters and continues to be a moral brake on the otherwise runaway sled of behavioral decadence that so characterizes our society. I think it is also clear that the Church contributed mightily, directly and indirectly, to the collapse of atheistic Communist rule in Poland, Czechoslovakia, and Hungary, which eventually helped bring down the Soviet Union itself. Stalin's mocking comment about the pope — "How many divisions does he have?" — has come back to haunt his heirs.

The Church has also attempted to expunge itself of its age-old official policy of anti-Semitism. The diplomatic recognition of the State of Israel by the Vatican is an historic admission of theological error on its part. The Church still has a long way to go in its relationship with the Jewish people, but the last 30 years have seen an unprecedented, positive change in its attitude and practice regarding the Jews. Maimonides stated in the 12th century that the Jews should view Christianity essentially as a conduit for Torah ideas — particularly messianism, but not necessarily limited to that — to help reach and influence the large non-Jewish world. I think that the Church is basically fulfilling that role in our time. It is almost as though, after floundering around for two millennia searching for its true purpose and mission, the Church has now gained a new confidence and self-identity in advancing what are basically Jewish ideas, goals, and attitudes in a skeptical, frightened, but yet approachable society. It is sad and ironic that many secular Jews are amongst the Church's most vehement critics in this endeavor. But Rome 2000 has positive aspects for us and warrants interested and hopeful monitoring on the part of Jewry.

The irony of Rome 2000 is that it never expected to have to share the stage of millennia celebration with Jerusalem 3000. The unexpected survival and vitality of Judaism and the Jewish people has spawned troubling theological problems for Church dogmatists. The problem of claiming to be exclusive in doctrine and all-knowing of G–d's will is that there is no room for interpreting unexpected historical phenomena. So Jerusalem 3000 may be proving slightly awkward in the planning of Rome 2000. But by now, I am hopeful that Rome realizes and accepts the fact that Jerusalem is not going to disappear. Its accommodation to that fact will make life easier not only for Jerusalem but for Rome itself. Meanwhile, we can safely say that Jerusalem will continue to abide by its ancient policy and belief, enunciated by the prophet Micah: "For every nation shall pursue the worship of its own faith, but as for us, we will continue to walk forth in the Name of the L–rd our G–d forever and ever."

Returning to Roots

Last July, in the shimmering sunlight so characteristic of the summer season in Israel, Yosef Fink and Rachamim Alsheich were buried in Jewish cemeteries in the Holy Land. The two were young Israeli soldiers who were kidnapped, tortured, and eventually executed by the Hizbollah terrorist organization in Lebanon 10 years earlier. Five years ago, their parents received news of very strong evidence proffered to Israeli authorities that clearly indicated their sons were no longer alive. The parents and families, indeed the entire country, came to accept the reality of the tragedy that Yosef Fink and Rachamim Alsheich were dead. But as long as their bodies were not returned for Jewish burial, the ritual periods of mourning, *shivah*, and *shloshim*, could not be observed, and their families, as well as the entire country, were still in emotional and spiritual limbo. The ancient and undying Jewish belief in the immortality of the soul and the holiness of the body, its host, is reflected in the ritual of *kever Yisrael* — underground burial in a Jewish cemetery. The struggle, cost, and effort expended by the State of Israel in retrieving the two bodies is a testimony to the sublime aspect of the state, which, in spite of all of its shortcomings and mistaken detours, always seems to lurch back to its roots — the understanding that it is not only a state for Jews but a Jewish state.

Small and Few — I

The song poem of *Haazinu* outlines the destiny and history of Israel are outlined. All of the fearsome events and great accomplishments of Jewish history are presented, albeit in a cryptic and sometimes difficult poetic fashion. Implicit in the words of Moses is the patent lesson that the Jewish people will remain small in numbers, both on an absolute and on a relative world scale. Moses quotes G-d as saying, "*Amarti afeihem* — I said I will diminish them," the word *afeihem* being derived from the Hebrew word *pe'ah,* meaning a corner, fringe, or remnant. The surviving number of Jews in the world today is only a small percentage of what the natural increase in population under normal circumstances would warrant. Josephus' estimate of over 10 million Jews in the Roman Empire in the first century C.E. should indicate a current Jewish population of over 500 million Jews! And yet the Jewish world population is not much larger today than Josephus' estimate almost two millennia ago. G-d's forecast of a numerically diminished nation of Israel has certainly come to pass, especially in this past century of World Wars I and II, Hitler, Stalin, and raging assimilation and intermarriage in the Western world. Thus, at first glance, this prophecy of Jewish paucity of numbers appears to be completely dire and negative. But the words of Torah have many facets to them, and to see the matter of *afeihem* as purely bad news would be a distorted vision of Jewish life and history.

Being small in numbers lends itself to creating a sense of importance and singularity in the group. The realization that there is a sense of urgency and responsibility in one's actions is enhanced by the comprehension that one is part of a very small group, and therefore every individual counts enormously in the fate and success of the group. Judaism is built upon the principle that "the entire universe was created only for me." There are billions of people in this world, but there is no one else who is *me,* who has my DNA, my personality, and my particular talents and potential contributions to society. Therefore, my responses to the challenges of life are of enormous importance to my Creator, my people, and humanity in general.

But, human nature being what it is, humans almost enjoy being lost in the crowd, in achieving blessed anonymity, thus believing they have escaped confrontation with their challenging destiny. The message of the song poem of *Haazinu* is that such a belief in the possibility of escaping from one's ultimate responsibility is fatuous and wildly wrong. The destiny of Israel is associated with each and every one of us, and our personal lives and achievements are measured against that standard. Part of the individual heavenly judgment that is so integral a part of the High Holy Days is based upon the relationship and contribution of a Jew to the society of Israel generally. And such contributions can occur only when one has a sense of individuality, uniqueness, and self-worth. The realization of the Jewish nation's small population certainly contributes to the formation of this attitude.

Another aspect of *afeihem* is the eternal nature of the people of Israel. Having survived all the evils of the past three millennia, the Jewish people have a unique view of humanity and its history — a view based upon this simple fact of survival. If there were massive numbers of Jews, the miracle of Jewish survival would not be impressive. The very smallness of Jewish numbers is a great testimony to the eternity of Israel and the Torah values it represents.

Small and Few – II

Moses is convinced that the people of Israel are on the threshold of entry into the Promised Land of Israel. He is convinced that the bickering, backbiting, and rebellious climate that marked the beginning of the Jewish journey through the Sinai desert is over. The sin of the Golden Calf, if not completely ameliorated, has receded into the background of Jewish consciousness, and the complaints against the manna (the heavenly bread that fell daily, except for on the Sabbath, in the Israelite camp in the desert) have apparently diminished. Moses feels invigorated by a sense of optimism and strength of purpose, of hope and conviction that the great promise of G–d to settle the Jews securely in the Land of Israel is close to fulfillment. His enthusiasm is reflected in the statement that he makes to his father-in-law, Jethro (Hobab): "We are now embarking on our journey to the place that the L–rd has promised to us. Come with us now and you will benefit from and with us, for the L–rd has promised well on behalf of Israel." Moses sees Jethro's presence in the camp of Israel as an essential component of the future success of the Jewish people, as well as a necessary morale booster in their current campaign to conquer the Land of Israel. Jethro has an historic opportunity to make a real difference in the story of Israel. He does not take advantage of it.

There are many reasons advanced by the Midrash for Jethro's behavior. Most of them express his legitimate excuses, if not downright noble calculations. But the bottom line is that Jethro leaves the camp of Israel in the Sinai desert and returns to his former home in Midian. And immediately after his defection, terrible problems and defeats cascade down upon the heads of Moses and Israel. The old complaints about the manna, the unrest that manifested itself in the unbelievably fond memories of Egyptian slavery and diet, the discouragement of an entire nation, and the unraveling of the program of entry into the Land of Israel all flow from Jethro's departure, though they are apparently in no way traceable to him. But such is life. A parent need only once disparage a child's ideas, and the light leaves that child's eyes, sometimes for a lifetime. A student's dream is often crushed by the rejection of a teacher or counselor. Anyone in public life is well aware of the deadening effect that the ever present nay-sayers have upon every project, no matter how necessary or admirable that project may be. It is always easier to say no, to stand aside, to retreat into one's own interests, to slip out of the room and the obligation. But this seemingly passive abstention from participation is a serious matter. As Jethro's example illustrates, unreasonable self-interest turns into nay-saying and eventually into desertion. In a time of struggle and national peril, desertion becomes a capital crime.

The Jewish nation is a small and impressionable one. It cannot really survive passive behavior on the part of its citizens. It is currently overwhelmed by desertions and defections. No matter how justified one's personal reasons may be, desertion is desertion. Intermarriage, anti-Jewish values and expressions, taking a lasseiz-faire attitude towards the dismantling of traditional Jewish life and values, all combine to create the climate of desertion that threatens to destroy American Jewry. So we should all stop running from ourselves, from our past, from our destiny, from our holy Torah and our own inherent spiritual greatness. Over the ages, few, if any, Jews named their children Jethro. The gaze of history is real and even harsh. No desertions allowed.

Hearing the Call

The prophet Isaiah, in exhorting Israel to realize its noble potential as a special and sanctified people, states: "Look to your father Abraham, and to Sarah, who has given birth to you. For I called him one and unique..." Abraham was certainly one and unique, but then again, who is not one and unique? All that we have learned in the recent past regarding DNA and genetic markers should be sufficient to convince everyone about human individuality and uniqueness. So why did Isaiah choose "one and unique" as the distinguishing feature of Abraham that demands our attention and emulation? In fact, "one and unique" is probably the most common feature, and therefore the least outstanding aspect, of an individual. I think that perhaps it is this very commonality of "one and unique" that the prophet wishes to stress in holding up Abraham as an example for all Jews.

The great Rebbe of Kotzk, Rabbi Menachem Mendel (Halpern) Morgenstern (19th-century Poland), in discussing the opening verse of *Lech Lecha*, stated that G–d's command to "go forth from your homeland, your birthplace, your family, and [follow Me] to a land that I will show you" was not addressed to Abraham alone. It was rather a general announcement, a Divine voice speaking to all men, advancing the challenge of a holy career and a life of human and godly service. In the Mishnah in *Avos* we find that "a heavenly voice emanates daily from Mount Sinai and proclaims: 'Woe to my creatures, for they insult my Torah so!'" There, too, the call from Sinai is a general one, audible and felt by all. But it is only the individual person — the "one and unique" — who truly feels the pain of the neglect of G–d and Torah in everyday life. So too, when Moses stumbles across the burning bush in the desert, the Rabbis point out that the bush was there for everyone to behold, not a private vision directed solely at Moses. But Moses was the "one and unique" person who reacted to the strange sight. He thereby launched his career as the teacher of Israel, and in fact of all mankind. Abraham heard the call to "go forth" and changed his life to accommodate this godly challenge. Others, just as "unique," did not attune their ears to hear G-d's call, or if they heard it, did not wish to alter their life-style to accommodate this new vision. It is because everyone had equal opportunity to become the "father of a multitude of nations," to be Abraham, and yet only Abraham responded positively to the call, that made him truly "one and unique."

In a world of conformity and correctness, where individuality and creativity often are stifled, unrewarded, and even criticized, we should remember our special oneness and uniqueness. Each of us is bidden to be Abraham and Sarah, for each of us is as "one and unique" as they were. The Rabbis of the Talmud taught us that we are to constantly ask ourselves: "When will my accomplishments and actions equal those of my forefathers?" In other words, when will I be Abraham or Sarah? It is only because of our commonality of being as "one and unique" as Abraham and Sarah that we can justify that question and attempt to achieve that goal. The G-d of Israel expects nothing less from us.

Survivors

All survivors of tragedies, personal or communal, are of necessity traumatized by the experience. "What happened?" "Why was I spared?" "What am I to do now to justify my survival?" These are the usual questions that arise to plague the survivor. And there are never any deeply satisfying answers. Noah was the original survivor, the prototype of millions who would follow him in escaping the sword of destruction, natural and manmade, over the long centuries of civilization. Even though he was warned by G–d and was aware of the terrible danger that his society faced, he nevertheless did not come to terms with the disaster that was imminent. The Rabbis of the Midrash stated that Noah himself did not enter the ark that he had built, even when the rains of the flood had already begun to fall, "until the waters reached his neck." The flood was a terrible tragedy that Noah was unable to prevent, and his feelings of inadequacy in facing it would haunt him for the rest of his days. In this respect Noah was the first of many survivors tortured by the past and forced to create a new future in its shadow.

The survivors of our century are not only those who somehow literally retained their lives and sanity during the Holocaust. In a true sense, Western society's pretensions of civilization and hopes for advancement are also survivors of the Holocaust. That tragedy haunts our century. The French Roman Catholic Church only now apologizes for its silence and collaboration in the extermination of the Jews of France 55 years ago. Its inner sense as a religious organization finally forced it to confront the past tragedy that it did little to prevent and nothing to remedy. That is a heavy burden to bear. The Swiss government and its bankers, all kicking and screaming and lying and hiding, have finally been flushed out and exposed. No one will ever think of Switzerland again merely in terms of the Alps, punctual trains, and neutrality. Survivors are always forced to confront their past. Only by dealing somehow, and I don't know exactly how, with past tragedy and error can society move forward to the hoped-for better tomorrow.

I had the opportunity to discuss with Rabbi She'ar Yashuv Cohen, chief rabbi of Haifa, his recent controversial visit to Vilna. He went on the invitation of the Lithuanian government to commemorate the 200th anniversary of Rabbi Elijah, the Gaon of Vilna. Many Jews, especially Lithuanian survivors of the Holocaust, objected to any Jewish participation in the event, due to the horrendous behavior of the Lithuanian people and government towards the Jews during the Holocaust and afterward. For various reasons, Rabbi Cohen did journey to Vilna for the event. He was invited to speak before the Lithuanian parliament. In his closing remarks to that legislature about their evil past, he read in Hebrew, and later translated for them in English, *Psalm* 124: "A Song of Ascents by David. Had it not been the L–rd Who was for us — let Israel declare it now. Had it not been the L–rd Who was for us when men rose up over us, then they would have swallowed us alive when their wrath burned against us. Then the waters would have washed us away when it had gone over our soul, as if toward a riverbed. Then it would have gone over our soul in the raging waters. Blessed be the L–rd, Who did not leave us as a prey for their teeth. Our soul escaped like a bird out of the snare of the hunters; the snare broke and we were free. Our help is in the Name of the L–rd, Who shapes heaven and earth." That pretty much says it all.

VIII
FAITH

Loyalty

Over the years I have spoken and lectured a number of times on the concept of loyalty. The topic was on my mind when I read that Peter O'Malley, the president of the Los Angeles Dodgers baseball franchise, announced that he was putting the team and its associated assets up for sale. Immediately, a number of die-hard Brooklyn Dodger fans, attempting to right the grievous wrong done to them 40 years ago when the late Walter O'Malley, Peter's father, moved the team from Brooklyn to Los Angeles, announced their intention to raise funds to buy the Dodgers and move them back to Brooklyn. But as of this writing, their attempt to galvanize public support and serious financial backing for their scheme has been met with thunderous silence and apathy. Loyalty to the Brooklyn Dodgers has apparently evaporated after one generation.

In general, our society has downgraded the quality of loyalty. Loyalty no long plays a great role in consumer brands choices, in sports management, players, and even fans, in political parties, candidates, and issues, and especially in marital and family situations. Loyalty to one's country, once proudly called patriotism, is no longer really in vogue. "My country, right or wrong — my country!" is an anachronism in our world. The sense of national cohesion that is necessary for societal progress has been replaced by a continuing conflict between differing special-interest groups that tends to divide the society. Loyalty has been replaced by narrow interests and unashamed selfishness. This malaise has affected every country in the world, ironically those that are true democracies in particular. The consequences of such attitudes are yet to be assessed, but I am convinced that this lack of loyalty does not augur well for the future of the democratic governments of the world.

Judaism has as its basis the quality of loyalty. And that loyalty is not limited just to relatives or people. The Talmud emphasizes that our father Abraham was loyal even to those inns where he had stayed when he was in modest circumstances, though he could later afford other accommodations. Respect and honor of parents is based on a sense of loyalty. Unfortunately, we are trained to give respect only as a matter of appreciation for others' services or kindnesses to us. Thus, when we no longer appreciate the other person — or worse, when we feel somehow wronged by that person, even if he is our spouse, parent, partner, or lifelong friend — we are free to disregard, denigrate, and even despise him.

Over my decades in the rabbinate, I have seen a slow erosion of respect for parents and spouses even amongst the most observant members of the American Jewish community. This may be the result of the relatively new influence of the American Jewish world. Our spouses and children have very high expectations, a sense of being automatically entitled to the American dream of a good car, a comfortable house, and winter and summer vacations. If these are provided, there is a strong sense of appreciation for the benefactors. If these material goods are not provided, however, there is a sense of anger and frustration, and many a family has been torn asunder by disappointment in parents. But the Torah commands us to honor and respect our parents in spite of their imperfections and our disappointment in them. The Torah is built upon loyalty, not on a sense of selfish appreciation. The prophets warn us against disloyalty to our spouses: "How have you allowed yourself to be a traitor to the wife of your youth?" The only way to build family, community, and national continuity is through a strong sense of loyalty. Wavering and ever changing life principles, current political correctness, and hedonistic behavior patterns, all serve to undermine any sense of continuity or moral strength in societies, Jewish and general.

I am impelled to relate the following anecdote: I delivered a lecture on this topic of loyalty to a large crowd in Miami Beach in 1996. In attendance was a young boy, now about 12 years old, who had attended some of my previous annual lectures. In the past, the boy would invariably come up to me after my lecture and ask me to autograph his book or notepad, which I did proudly. This year at my lecture, I was introduced by Alan Viengrad, a former offensive lineman and Super-Bowl-ring-wearer for the Dallas Cowboys. After my inspired words on the topic of loyalty, the young man made a beeline for the champion athlete and asked *him* for his autograph, completely ignoring me! I guess I didn't make the point emphatically enough. But I hope that you will understand and consider this matter of loyalty and its importance in our personal and communal lives.

Public Piety and the Jewish Problem

One of the great blessings of American society is the absence of a state church. The Bill of Rights, attached to the Constitution of the United States, guarantees freedom of religion. But it equally guarantees freedom *from* religion. Even though our money proclaims, "In G–d We Trust," the Supreme Court of the United States has zealously protected the prohibition against public governmental displays of religion. One would therefore think that the United States should be the most secular of all Western societies. But just the opposite is true. Consider these items gleaned from an article appearing in *The New York Times* on December 4, 1994:

1) "A poll released last year by a consortium of social science research centers showed that, among the dozen technologically advanced nations surveyed [I wonder if Israel was included — BW], belief in G–d was highest in the United States and Ireland … Americans [scored] higher than most in church attendance, belief in an afterlife, and the conviction that G–d truly cares about individuals."

2) An increasing number of sports heroes give a public demonstration of their religious belief while performing in their chosen sport.

3) An amendment to the Constitution protecting public prayer in school was a promise of the platform of the winning party in the last general election in the United States.

4) "Outright secularism never gained much of a constituency in the country at large … America is a nation where public expression of religion seem[s] always to be in season."

In the time-honored fashion of Jews following the trends of the general society, a significant change has now occurred in American Jewry in its attitude toward public displays of religious identification and belief. Originally, there was only one trend in American Jewish society. It was represented by the older, more affluent, leadership establishment, the professional-Jewish-organization "Jewish Leaders" group. It was always opposed, and remains opposed, to all public expressions of any religion, especially Judaism. They were joined in this attitude by the Eastern European Jewish immigrants, many of whom were Orthodox and observant and valued Jewish education for their young, but who nonetheless opposed any public demonstration of their Jewishness. Growing up "*frum*" in Chicago half a century ago meant wearing a cap but never a *yarmulke* in public, sneaking home from college or work on winter Friday afternoons but never confronting the professor or the boss with the issue, and keeping a low public profile on all matters of Jewish observance. There were relatively few "visible Jews," and those who did exist were seen as being either European-born rabbis who did not adapt to the New World or fanatics who would never be able to function in a modern society. Jews therefore abhorred all public displays of religion, for if no public display was the rule for all of American society, they would be safely American in casting off the trappings of their faith.

Over the last few decades, a new trend has developed in American Jewish life. Jews who are observant are more publicly aggressive about their observance. The younger generation demands bearded rabbis, black hats or knitted *kippos* — both of which are symbolic statements of Jewishness — on the heads of their children and students in the street, active religious Jewish participation in public and political life, the raising of strictly Jewish issues to the forefront of public agendas, Sabbath-observing programs, internships, and employment and advancement opportunities, communal zoning laws that allow and protect "*eiruvin*," "*shtibels*," and "*mikvaos*," and sanctioned

"*Minchah*" stops on public expressways. This trend is not limited to the Orthodox camp alone, though the Orthodox are its
most vocal supporters. Public half-page advertisements spon-
sored by secular Jewish organizations on "What Being Jewish
Means to Me," full-page advertisements in the general press on
Jewish topics, holidays, issues, and politics, large and enormously popular Holocaust museums in Washington, Los
Angeles, and now in New York City, fierce and public lobbying
on behalf of the State of Israel, Soviet Jewry, Ethiopian Jews,
etc., are all the norm today. This from an American Jewish society which was silent to a fault during the Holocaust! It is safe to
say that American Jewry has come out of hiding in this closing
decade of the 20th century.

England is five hours ahead and 50 years behind the United
States. In a brilliant article in the December 12, 1994 issue of
New Yorker Magazine, Calvin Trillin writes of the controversy
engulfing British society and its Jewish constituency concern-
ing the attempt to construct an *eiruv* in a predominantly Jewish
(though not observant) London suburb. An "English bird-lover
[complaining to the local zoning board was] concerned that the
wires [of the *eiruv*] could be a hazard to his feathered friends
("our first priority must be toward the birds"). Trillin points out
that the root of the mainly Jewish opposition to the *eiruv* is really based on the Jews' perception of themselves in England.
"English Jews often feel what has been described as a sort of
otherness, a feeling common to longtime boarders. Traditionally, the way they dealt with that otherness was to keep their
heads down." But now a new generation has arisen in the Jewish society in England that "finds it stifling to tiptoe up the stairs
when family discussions are going on in the parlor." They say:
"Our parents' generation are used to Jews being invisible. The
eiruv threatens their invisibility. In the context of the way English Jews have been Jews, some [of us younger people] think
that the only way to be more Jewish is to be more observant."
The rabbi leading the struggle for the *eiruv* summed up the

matter succinctly: "Resistance ... will melt away only after the *eiruv* is established and people realize that physically it hardly exists. It's the concept that is disturbing."

In the pluralistic and open society that is developing in the Western world, there are grave dangers and glorious opportunities for Jewish life and expression. As in all matters, moderation and wisdom, patience and good counsel will be necessary for success. The freedom to practice Judaism openly, without governmental hindrance and overt danger, should serve as a great aid in revitalizing Jewish life the world over. Jews continue to have a unique opportunity to be the conscience of civilization. In our time, that opportunity is no longer restricted to the privacy of our homes, but rather can be displayed in the public arenas of modern life. History will judge us by how well we exploited this opportunity.

Faith — Abundant and Overabundant

As a rabbi and a Jew who attempts to live a traditional Torah life, I would never have the temerity to criticize a human being's overabundance of faith. Nevertheless, I feel that one of the primary ills that afflict society — both Jewish and non-Jewish — in our time is a surfeit of confidence in faith. Not necessarily faith in the Creator or faith in His Divine scheme for the universe and mankind, but rather a more sinister and dangerous type of faith — faith in our own infallibility and rectitude of purpose and action. One of the qualities that G–d demands of man, as enunciated by the prophet Micah, is "to walk humbly with your G–d." I think that "walking humbly" may mean having perfect faith in G–d while maintaining a healthy skepticism about one-self and one's view of matters of life. The arrogance of certitude is the precursor of persecution and intolerance of others. Only G–d exists in certainty. Man is doomed to an existence of doubts, crises, and mysteries. This reality alone should nudge us towards walking "humbly" with our G–d.

One of the great gifts of intellect is the ability to judge things rationally and foresee the future consequences of behavior. The Rabbis in *Ethics of the Fathers* stated the case succinctly: "Who is the wise man? He who foresees what will be born from his actions." But sometimes an overabundant faith, a tinge of irrationality, overcomes the otherwise judicious believer. He becomes convinced somehow that he knows G–d's mind and will. He is certain that his own will, his personal perspective on the situation, is also G–d's opinion. Therefore, his overabundant faith in his own rectitude renders him infallible, a most difficult and dangerous situation for any human being to find himself in.

Is that not the true analysis of the terrible deed of Yigal Amir in his assassination of Yitzhak Rabin? "G–d told me to do it," he said. More realistically, he told G–d to agree with his crazed action. But G–d is not obligated to accept man's opinion of the matter — any man, no matter how wise and holy he may be. Amir certainly did not intend to make Peres prime minister of Israel or to speed up the transfer of autonomous power and Holy Land territory to Arafat. However, any moment of rational thought would have made him realize the terrible counterproductivity of his behavior. But if one is convinced that G–d talks to him, and that G–d's will in political and world affairs is known to him in perfect faith, then there is no room to apply the dictum of the Rabbis regarding a truly wise man.

The great rabbi of the Second Temple Era, Rabban Yochanan ben Zakai, made the fateful decision regarding Jewish survival soon after Jerusalem had been burned and the Temple stood in ruins. Guaranteed a favorable response to any reasonable request that he would make from the Roman Emperor Vespasian, the rabbi asked for the safety of the great yeshivah of Yavneh and its scholars and students. He felt that Jewish survival would thereby be assured, even under the terrible stress of Roman persecution. Yet the Talmud tells us that, decades later on his deathbed, Rabban Yochanan ben Zakai was still uncertain about G–d's opinion of his choice and policy. This, after it was now apparently clear to all on earth that Yavneh had indeed become the salvation of Torah and Israel, Rabban Yochanan felt that it was still too early to assess what the G–d of history thought about the matter. Rabban Yochanan ben Zakai was a man of perfect and abiding faith in his Creator and in the Torah of Israel. However, he did not suffer from the plague of possessing an overabundant faith that would lead him to automatically assume that his behavior and policy were certainly G–d's will as well.

The problem of arrogant and overabundant faith is not limited to adherents of organized religion solely. One of the great disappointments of the modern world is the failure of secular governments, universities, and societies to practice the one most valuable ingredient of the secularist code — a healthy sense of skepticism about one's self and one's policies. In an out-standing essay titled "Secularism's Blind Faith" which appeared in the September 1995 issue of *Harper's Magazine*, Peter Marin, himself an avowed political liberal and secularist non-believer, raises the specter of the overabundant faith of modern secularism itself. He states: "The great dream at the heart of modern American secularism has always been that religion would slowly wither away, giving way, as it did so, to a morality rooted not in a fear of G–d or the hope of heaven but in reflection, a sense of kinship, and a belief in the common good. Values once maintained through oppression or fear would rise naturally from human reason, instinct, and sympathy. The religious divisions and hatred separating us from one another would disappear, and the senses of gratitude and awe traditionally felt for G–d would be transferred to the human world and provide a foundation for a universalized community. As we know, none of this came to be, or is likely to come to be. The struggle to live ethically without G–d has left us not with the just and moral order we imagined but with disorder and confusion." Marin continues: "Something has gone radically wrong with secularism. The problem has more than its share of irony, for secularism, in the end, has converted itself into a kind or religion. Our hallowed tradition of skepticism and tolerance has grown into its near opposite, and it now partakes of precisely the same arrrogance, the same irrationality and passion for certainty, the same pretense to unquestioned virtue against which its powers were once arrayed. In the desperate way we cling to [our secular] belief, in our contempt for those who do not believe what we believe, secularism has, indeed, taken on the trappings of a faith — and a narrow one at that." But perhaps Marin's most telling statements are these: "The attitudes I am describing — a passion for totalizing thought, a conviction that we know better than others what is good for them — cut across almost the entire range of contemporary secularism. They're present, obviously, in the Marxist notions of the new man (and also in the secularist Zionist notion of the new Jew — BW), in the speech and behavior codes now enacted on campuses, and in the fury with which abortion-rights defenders denounce as charlatans or knaves all those who persist in thinking of the fetus as a person and alive.

"All of the positions I've named may indeed be defensible on one ground or another, but what's important is that they're held with a monstrous certainty, one that first assumes a tone of self-righteousness and then the form of coercion or tyranny. The astonishing thing about all this is that such certainty, such freedom from self-doubt, persists at the heart of secularism even after the past century, after countless examples of the ways in which predominantly secularist ideologies — I am thinking here of Marxism, Stalinism, the Maoists in China — have failed to produce the promised results. What we should have learned has something to do with fallibility, with humility, with the endless human capacity for error. It ought to have sent us rushing back to examine the fundamental assumptions we've made about the world, the pretty castles and palaces we've etched in the air. We know now, or ought to know, that men are as ready to kill in G–d's absence as they are in His name; that reason, like faith, can lead to murder; that the fanaticism long associated with religion was not born there, but has its roots deeper in human nature."

There is a well-written, provocative, cantankerous, sometimes outrageous book on the market called *In Defense of Elitism*, by William A. Henry III. Most of the current trends in "correct" political thinking and programs are skewered in this work. The basic premise of the book is that modern government, universities, media, and society have all succumbed to the virus of certainty occasioned by overabundant faith. We gleefully allow ourselves the luxury of rewriting history, debunking heroic figures, judging past events and people by current standards of correctness. In the process, we discard hard-learned lessons of history and society about the inequality of talent and skill, confusing those ineradicable human differences with the goal of equality of opportunity, which is a far different matter, all because we are convinced that our generation knows better. We have equalized everyone in this new faith of ours, accomplishing what Senator Daniel Patrick Moynihan described as "defining deviancy down." Life and history teach that not all people, cultures, faiths, governments, and teachings are equal in terms of their contributions to civilization and human welfare; but in our faith that we know everything, we prefer to whistle past the graveyard rather than face up to the rational realities of life as they are.

Arthur Schlesinger, Jr., the noted historian and confidant of presidents, wrote in his 1991 book, *The Disuniting of America*, as follows: "Let us by all means teach black history, African history, woman's history, Hispanic history, Asian history. But let us teach them as history, not as filiopietistic commemoration. The purpose of history is to promote not group self-esteem, but understanding of the world and the past, dispassionate analysis, and perspective, respect for divergent cultures and traditions, and unflinching protection for those ideas of tolerance, democracy, and human rights that make free historical inquiry possible." In other words, history should teach us a realistic approach, not one based upon overabundant faith in our own truths and perspectives.

The Torah bids us to be "whole, trusting, almost naive, with the L–rd your G–d." This dictate presupposes a sense of humility, a questioning of our own motives and actions, a healthy skepticism regarding the ultimate wisdom and consequences of our policies and actions. It bids us to have true trust and faith in our Creator, whose guidance and control is omnipresent but at the same time inscrutable and mysterious. If we follow such a path, much of the pain and damage of excessive behavior, extremist actions, and rash judgments will be spared us. We will then be "whole, trusting, almost naive" in our faith in the G–d of history, Who has preserved us as Jews till this very day; and we will have made a most important contribution to the furtherance of the meaningful enhancement of world society.

Mea Culpa

As we all know from personal experience, three of the most difficult words in the English language to pronounce when strung together are: "I am sorry." The furor over the lack of an official public apology from Japan over its behavior in World War II clouded the commemoration ceremonies marking the 50th anniversary of the end of that terrible conflict. One of the great mysteries of human psychology is why admitting past error is so difficult and gut wrenching. Apparently, it is an act so ego deflating that many people and governments consider it beyond their ability. But the sad truth about life is that we can learn from our past mistakes, and the necessity for some form of atonement — at least a verbal statement of culpability and apology — is the beginning of such a learning experience.

The tragic and murderous history of the Soviet Union in our century can serve as another example. Faced by the terrible failure of its collectivization agricultural policy in the early 1930s, the Soviet government responded to the discontent of its party and citizens by an even greater terror campaign in 1936-38. Boris Pasternak, the great Russian writer, reviews the situation, albeit somewhat simplistically, in his book *Doctor Zhivago*: "Collectivization was an erroneous and unsuccessful measure, and it was *impossible to admit the error* (italics mine — BW). To conceal the failure, people had to be cured, by every means of terrorism, of the habit of thinking and judging for themselves, and forced to see what did not exist, to assert the very opposite of what their very eyes told them. This accounts for the unexampled cruelty of the Yezhov (the NKVD chief in charge of the purges and terror of the period who was later purged himself by Stalin) period." The danger of being unable to admit and apologize for error, public or private, is that one is forced to deny the existence of such error. If no error ever occurred, then there is no lesson that can be learned from the experience and no improvement in life is possible.

In December 1894, a French military court-martial found Captain Alfred Dreyfus guilty of treason and sentenced him to life imprisonment on Devils' Island. The evidence against Dreyfus, a hapless and uncharismatic Jewish officer on the French General Staff during the Franco-Prussian War of 1870, was fabricated and false. The Dreyfus affair embroiled French society for the next decade, splitting the country and greatly weakening its military resolve. It was also the catalyst for Herzl's forming the World Zionist Organization. The falseness of the charges against Dreyfus was eventually proved to the satisfaction of all except the French General Staff. Last September, 101 years after the French military convicted an innocent man on the basis of evidence that it knew to be false, the French General Staff finally admitted its guilt and apologized for its base behavior. The arrogance of military officers in high positions precluded the honesty which alone could have strengthened French military credibility in both world wars and in the many losing colonial battles of France in this century. Generals rarely if ever admit error, accept blame, or say "I'm sorry." But I imagine that the admission of culpability in the sordid Dreyfus affair, even at this late date, is to be appreciated and commended.

The first component, the foundation, so to speak, of the Jewish attitude towards repentance, self-improvement, and emotional and spiritual growth is the ability to admit past error. Feeling regret for past actions and shortcomings is universal; saying so is much less common. In 40 years in the rabbinate, I have learned, painfully and often unwillingly, that outside criticism can be a positive thing. But in interpersonal and communal relationships, it is essential to express one's regrets in order to profit from the criticism. And the ability to express our regret for acts committed against others who are weaker, smaller, or unimportant to us is part of this formula. How many times have I heard students and children complain that, even when proven wrong, their teachers or parents refuse to admit their error and apologize to them! In not expressing regret, a noble opportunity to forge lifetime loyalties between teachers and students, or parents and their children, is lost. One who had a great spirit makes allowance for his errors and owns up to them.

The greatness of the holy day of Yom Kippur lies in the recitation of its confessional prayers. Our sins are forgiven on that day by our Creator, but only because we have *said* that we have erred and that we are sorry for our backsliding.

The basic opinion of the majority of the great scholars of Israel is that the recitation of our "mea culpa" is the necessary condition for G–d's forgiveness of us. This is true in human affairs as well. The psychological pain of having to say "I am sorry" is far easier to bear than the physical and emotional consequences of not having done so.

G–d in the Home and in the Heart

It is noteworthy that the book of the *Chumash* that deals mainly with the ritual and laws of sacrifices, purity, and Temple service begins with the word *"vayikra"* — "And G–d called out." The basis of all services that require sacrifice, inhibition, holiness, and dedication is the feeling of performing an eternal and noble act. That feeling is not easily achieved and maintained when there is no supernatural, holy aura attached to it. In an increasingly secular eternal society, such a feeling of exalted sacrificial service has become a very rare commodity indeed. It is not merely a matter of volunteerism and altruism that lies at the heart of doing good, of undertaking tasks that will certainly be expensive to us in terms of time, effort, and wealth; it is rather the feeling that one is participating in a matter of cosmic importance and eternal value that truly drives our sense of sacrifice and service. To experience that holy feeling, one must believe that "G–d called out" to him or her, and that he continues to "call out" constantly in encouragement and strength, reinforcing our commitment to spiritual sacrifices and making us worthy of being His servants and people.

The sense of the presence of G–d in the lives of humans is one of the basic principles of Jewish faith. In all Jewish life over the centuries, G–d was always a presence in the Jewish home. I have always felt that part of the reason that Jewish family life over the ages was more stable, healthy, and less pathological than in the general society was because of the realization that G–d is part of the household. Therefore, people behaved more cautiously, more kindly, in a more circumspect fashion, because they did not want to "embarrass" themselves in front of their heavenly "Guest." An analogy may be made to how a family behaves when grandparents come to visit for a while. Everyone is on his best behavior because of the realization that there is a powerful and influential force present in the house and that it must be reckoned with. Well, Jews always thought that G–d was a regular visitor in their homes and hearts, and therefore took the Divine Presence into account in their everyday behavior and speech. They were convinced that G–d was constantly there and that He "called out" to them in a demanding, challenging, comforting, encouraging, and inspiring way.

Even though ritual observance of *mitzvos* is a necessity for the survival of the Jewish home and nation, it alone does not produce a sense of the immanent presence of the Almighty in our lives. It is the sad hallmark of current Jewish life that the L–rd somehow does not really figure in our lives, no matter how much pious lip-service we pay to His presence. And to compound this situation, all of the ills of the general society have seeped into Jewish family life: Divorce, substance abuse, verbal and physical abuse, generational alienation, and dysfunctional families have all become part of our domestic scene. There are myriad causes for this deterioration in Jewish family life, but there can be no doubt that the loss of the sense of G–d "calling out" to us is part of the problem. And it seems that even though our schools and *yeshivos* are successful in imparting Jewish knowledge, they have been far less successful in transmitting a sense of the spirituality of the traditional Jewish life-style, the intuitive awareness of G–d's presence in our homes. We must therefore retrain our ears and our hearts to realize that G–d is "calling out" to us and learn to respond patiently and truthfully to that call. It is a call which summons us to sacrifice and to be on our best behavior, but it also summons us to greatness, accomplishment, and inner peace.

Unanswered Prayer

Moses attempts to tear down the gates of heaven in an onslaught of prayer to G–d that is described in the Torah portion of *Va'eschanan*. He appeals to G–d to allow him entry into the Land of Israel. He marshals every cogent argument, logical and emotional, to sway the Divine Judge to decide in his favor. There is no doubt that all of Israel prayed with and for him as well, urgently wishing Moses to lead them into the Promised Land. The Rabbis tell us in the Midrash that Moses offered up 515 (the numerical value of the Hebrew word "*va'eschanan*") forms of prayer, influencing even the angels to hearken to his plea. But all to no avail. G–d refuses to allow him to enter the Land of Israel. More than that, G–d prevents any further discussion of the matter: "Do not continue to speak to Me further regarding this matter," He tells Moses in awful finality. Moses' prayers, no matter how fervent, sincere, and justified, will not be answered. How does Moses deal with that? How does mankind generally deal with the ever present and troubling problem of unanswered prayer?

Moses' reaction to G–d's refusal is a combination of disappointment, resignation, acceptance, and renewal. In short, it is the intelligent, quintessential reaction of humans — believing, faithful, good humans — to unanswered prayer. For prayer is a very personal thing, narrowly focused, offered up almost in a vacuum, without consideration for its consequences upon others and upon G–d's plan for this world. There is a rule in the Talmud that states: "The rule of one leader is not allowed to impinge on the rule of his successor, even for the breadth of a hair." Part of G–d's refusal to heed Moses' prayer is that the time of Joshua had arrived, and that in the heavenly plan of Israel and mankind "a generation goeth and a generation cometh." The L–rd allows no one to overstay his welcome on this earth. The next generation and the next leader are always waiting to enter. The wise man, Moses, realizes this, and though personally disappointed, he accepts G–d's wisdom. Joshua is not Moses — the Jewish people will say that Joshua is only the moon while Moses was the sun — but that is the inexorable way of the world. And Moses bows before the eternal will of G–d.

Perhaps it is Moses' very greatness that makes him unfit to lead the next generation. Every generation needs heroes but not demigods. We are witness in our century to the deadening hand of infallible leaders and gigantic, bigger-than-life personalities. The new generation of Jews in the desert, who never knew Moses at the beginning of his career and no longer saw him as a fellow mortal, would be in danger of idolizing him and worshipping him. The Torah is careful to prevent the deification of humans, which is one of the most basic Jewish objections to the Christian faith. Answering Moses' personal prayer would have had a negative effect on all society, present and future. The L–rd therefore remains apparently unmoved by Moses' prayers, because, in heavenly terms, there are many other considerations involved in any situation, considerations unseen and unrecognized by mortals, no matter how great they may be.

I do not have the temerity to claim to speak for G–d. But I think that the concept of prayer, one of the greatest gifts that G–d has bestowed on man, must always include the realization of the possibility that it will go unanswered. And prayer unanswered is part of the trial of faith and the inscrutability of the will of the Creator. "For my thoughts are not your thoughts," says G–d to the prophet Isaiah. The example of Moses and his prayer is therefore most instructive to all of us in our lives and trials. It should serve to strengthen our faith, even when life and its events disappoint us.

Song

Song is a wonderful thing. In fact, music in Jewish tradition has always been considered a spiritual matter, not just a matter of ears and throat. Song comes in many shapes and forms, and though musicality itself is a universal human trait, the type and sound of song is always individual, ranging from society to society and culture to culture. In the description of Israel's miraculous salvation from the army of the Egyptian Pharaoh, the Torah records for us the joyous song of triumph and thanksgiving offered by Moses and the Israelites. Because of this song, the Sabbath when the Torah reading of this song occurs is called *Shabbos Shirah* — the Sabbath of Song. In most synagogues throughout the Jewish world, this song of Moses is sung to a special melody that helps to make this great event of Jewish history so memorable.

Song is always an inspired and talent-laden phenomenon. However, it is not always a spontaneous event. Composers work long and hard to create songs, and performers rehearse and train in order to sing them. Yet there are moments in history when song springs forth spontaneously as a reaction to events. The song at the Red Sea is an example of this type. It was unplanned and flowed from the depth of the Jewish people's emotion at witnessing G–d's miraculous intervention on their behalf.

But even the strongest of emotions eventually weakens and pales. We recite this Song of Moses daily in our prayers, and no matter how great our concentration, it is obvious that we can never again capture the heights of fervor that our ancestors reached on the Red Sea when they sang this Song of Moses. Spontaneous song is exciting and stirring, but it is also inimitable. Not so with planned and composed song; it is always measured and delineated, and therefore can be replicated at will. The great example of this type of composed song is to be found in the other song of Moses recorded in the portion of *Haazinu*. That song, however, is *the song* of the Jewish people. The Torah itself commands the Jewish people of all generations to "learn that song, place it in their mouths" so that it will become "the witness" for all time of the eternal covenant between G–d and Israel. Thus, the planned, non-emotional, composed song of *Haazinu* somehow towers over the inspired and spontaneous beauty of the song of *Beshalach*.

It is that way in life and faith generally. Spontaneity and emotion are always attractive and exciting. We all want to be swept away on an emotional high, to feel spiritually exhilarated and musically moved. But such feelings are always short lived. No one can live indefinitely on a diet of continued emotion and spontaneous song. Rather, the measured cadence of disciplined life, of a rational and historic view of personal and Jewish life, of a traditional Torah life and value system, as unexciting as that may appear to uninitiated outsiders, is the way of permanent song and eternal life. Jews recite the Song of Moses, sung at the Red Sea, daily as a reminder of G–d's munificence to Israel. But Jews should remember constantly, in their psyches and souls, great song of *Haazinu*. For it is that song that truly defines us, reminds us of our past, and guides our attitudes and actions as a holy people. We should be reminded not only of the spontaneous song, but of the measured and composed song of Moses as well. That way we will always be guaranteed a life of song.

Does It Have a Prayer?

Part of the new "contract with America" which the Republican Party so skillfully proposed in winning the congressional elections in November 1994 was the promise to restore prayer as an integral part of the public school day, by means of a constitutional amendment initiative. This set me to reminiscing about my experiences with prayer when I attended public school in Chicago half a century ago.

The school I attended was Victor F. Lawson Elementary School, then located on Homan Avenue in the overwhelmingly Jewish Lawndale district on the west side of Chicago. My memories of school begin with the second grade, taught by an Irish Protestant disciplinarian, a spinster named Miss McCarthy. We began every day with the singing of the national anthem (that was my first hint about my many imperfections, for though my mother had assured me that I was a great singer, Miss McCarthy told me just to mouth the words since I was incurably tone deaf). Next came the Pledge of Allegiance to the flag of the United States, and then the L–rd's Prayer, with the name of the Christian savior omitted from the text in deference to the fact that 34 of the 35 students in the class were Jewish. I noticed that the students were not much affected by the prayer interlude since it was a rote routine, mainly unintelligible, and not at all meaningful in the scheme of the school day. I personally felt completely out of the prayer loop since my mother, a formidable person in her own right, had given me strict instructions to ignore the whole matter!

I was reminded of this long-past elementary school horror by an article that appeared on the op-ed page of *The New York Times*. The article was authored by David Klinghoffer, the editor of *National Review*, and was entitled "Give Us This Day Our Daily Pablum." Klinghoffer makes the case convincingly that a daily school prayer, nondenominational in nature and language and structured to offend no one, would be a hollow prayer that would eventually prove counterproductive to the values that the proponents of school prayer wish to introduce into the public-education system of our country. But his article then branches off to discuss an even broader and more important issue — the nature of prayer itself. A substantial portion of the article follows:

"American churches fail to inspire congregants, and so lose them, in direct proportion to the degree that the church compromises with the 'modern' world and makes few real demands of the congregants in order to avoid offending them. I know best the woes of the Reform movement, the liberal wing of Judaism, for which compromise with the world is a principle of faith. Reform dispensed with the Siddur more than a century ago. Since 1975, Reform Jews have prayed from a book with the title *Gates of Prayer*, from which the Engel prayer might easily have been extracted: A–mighty G–d, we acknowledge our dependence upon Thee, and we beg Thy blessings upon us, our parents, our teachers and our country. [This prayer was proposed by the New York Board of Regents for recitation in the New York public school system — BW].

"None of my classmates at Reform Hebrew school took this colorless document seriously, full as it was of soft words that asked little of us and seemed to request of G–d only that He be nice. We stopped attending Reform services when we got to college. Today, the only Jewish denomination able to hold on to its young people is Orthodoxy.

"After all, authentic religions have distinct ideas about what G–d is and what He demands. Authentic prayer reflects this, which is why it so often seems, to outside eyes, so strange, even dangerous. Kids know false prayer when they see it. And false prayer, like the one in Engel [quoted above], has in mind not the supernatural, transcendent relation of G–d to man but the mundane, political relation of man to man. It seeks to convey only as much truth as it feels confident won't offend anybody."

Prayer is possibly the most difficult of all religious rituals for modern man to relate to and perform. It requires, in Jewish practice, daily habit, a commitment of time (the rarest possession of modern man), and concentrated effort. It is discomforting, for it declares, more than any other religious act, our lack of control over our lives and fate, and it casts grave doubts over our cherished sureties. It is sobering, humbling, even frightening, to have to say daily in a public forum: "What are we? What is our life? What is our piety? What is our righteousness? What is our salvation? Our strength? Our might? What shall we say before You, O L–rd our G–d and G–d of our fathers? Are not all the mighty men as nothing before You, the wise as if without knowledge, the men of understanding as if without discernment? For most of their accomplishments are empty, and the days of their lives are vanity, and man's preeminence over beasts is nought, for all is vanity. Yet we are Your people, the children of Your covenant, the descendants of Abraham, Isaac, and Jacob ... It is therefore our duty to thank, praise, glorify You, to bless and to sanctify and to offer praise and thanksgiving to Your Name. Happy and fortunate are we! How goodly is our portion, how pleasant our lot, how glorious our heritage! Happy are we who, early and late, morning and evening, twice daily declare: Hear O Israel, the L–rd is our G–d, the L–rd is One!" This is an authentic prayer!

It is prayer more than anything else that defines our relationship with G–d and our true religious nature. Through prayer G–d becomes familiar to us, much as a parent becomes familiar to newborn children by habit and association. Once that relationship with G–d is established, we are able to insert into our prayer private requests, personal hopes and dreams, commitments, even past regrets and future promises. Prayer then becomes immediate, practical, and beneficial, no matter what G–d's response appears to be. However, in the impersonal, no-fault, obligation-free, amoral society of the modern age, when prayer is pablum and must be politically correct, no personal relationship with G–d is ever possible. It becomes pretentious and arrogant to attempt to reach Him when we are in need, after having ignored Him for most of our lives. A child (and we always remain children to our parents) can ask a parent for anything at any time, for such is the nature of their bonding. A person can rarely, if ever, do the same with a total stranger or even a casual acquaintance.

I noticed a striking example of the beneficial phenomenon of prayer in an article by Gillian Sender, published in the *Journal of Ecology and Natural Living* and reprinted in *The Jerusalem Post*. Titled "Healing With Prayer," the article reflects the premise that prayer works. It states: "People know that prayer works because their own lives reflect it working." In 1986, well-known internist and author, Dr. Larry Dossey, learned of a carefully controlled study which showed that patients in a coronary heart unit who were prayed for on a daily basis apparently did better on average than patients not receiving prayers. In this study, 400 patients who were admitted to the cardiology care unit at San Francisco General Hospital were divided into two groups. All of them received state-of-the-art treatment. However, the names of half the people were given out to various prayer groups in the Bay Area. No one was told how to pray. The only instructions provided were simply to pray for the people whose names had been assigned to them. It was a double blind study; no one in the group, neither the doctors, nurses, or patients knew who was being prayed for and who wasn't. At the end of the study, it looked as if the people who received prayers had been given some sort of special medication. There were fewer deaths in this group. No one in the prayed-for group needed to be put on the mechanical ventilator. But in the unprayed-for group, there were 12 people who needed the ventilator. They needed more potent medicine than the other group, and there were more deaths among them. The results of this study: If you take prayer into the hospital, it saves lives and makes people better.

Dr. Dorsey stated: "I assure you that if this was a study of some new type of medication, the results would have been received as a modern medical breakthrough. [Yet] most doctors think that even though the results seem positive, somehow it must be phony. Common sense tells us that prayer can't work. They [doctors] go into this area with their minds basically made up and they don't look at the information. So the information gets ignored." The article concludes by stating, "The bottom line: Prayer works."

Prayer works for those who pray and for those who are prayed for. Real, definitive, authentic prayer provides a release from earthly bonds and allows one to know himself in relation to his Creator. However, ersatz prayer is, in my opinion, worse than no prayer. I often listen to a Friday afternoon Sabbath prayer service from Temple Emmanuel in New York, which is broadcast on an FM station in the New York area. The organ, the choir, the pomposity and chilling formality of the leaders of the service all make the affair dreary and sterile. I keep listening because I hope that someday they'll catch on and make it more meaningful, more Jewish. So far, in 20 years, the program has never had one note of spontaneity, feeling, or commitment. The message is always soothing, undemanding, never challenging, and basically nonsectarian in its religious approach. But the part of the service that always makes me saddest is when the leader calls for a moment's meditation while the organ music fills the sanctuary and bids everyone "to pray as the heart prompts"!

Well, prayer is not what the "heart prompts." It is a wrenching experience, required daily of us in order that we have some perspective on our lives, our responsibilities, and our destinies. It contains hard words, tough commitments, expensive promises, long-term implications. It is the expression of man's search for the sublime and should never be demeaned by being turned into platitudes for political correctness or social engineering. Jews recite the following verse from *Psalms* at the beginning of their formal silent prayer service: "L–rd, open my lips, and may my mouth recite Your praises." That's no pablum. That's prayer.

P.S. The following item appeared recently in *The Washington Post*: "It has been tradition that Congress has its own full-time chaplains — one for the House and one for the Senate — paid to open each session with a prayer. Now ... some Republican budget-slashers are talking of cutting [out] ... the salaries for the chaplains and their assistants ... In deciding the chaplains' future, the conservative Republican majority could find itself torn: Should it cut perks wherever possible or preserve Congress' most visible living symbol of religious piety?" Perhaps through intensive, personal, and meaningful prayer, our Congressmen will gain insight and inspiration to deal with this problem.

Nongenetic Faith

Moses is embarked on a mission that he never really wanted to accept. When G–d called him to eternal greatness in the encounter at the burning bush, Moses' response was less than enthusiastic. "Send someone else," was his reaction to the Divine proposition. And when his original reluctance was apparently vindicated by Pharaoh's hard-hearted refusal to let Israel go, and in fact he intensified the pain of the Jewish slaves, Moses in effect told G–d, This is what I thought would happen." The response of G–d, as recorded in the Torah, is illuminating and vexing at the same time. To paraphrase, G–d says, "I appeared to Abraham, Isaac, and Jacob, also under very trying and dis-heartening circumstances, and in a more modified form of revelation than I used with you, and yet they never complained of their difficulties or faltered in their devotion to their godly mission." The Rabbis of the Midrash comment that "what was once present and then lost — the steadfast faith of our forefathers — is not easily found again."

The ability to deal with adversity is one of the great tests of life. This is especially true for adversity that comes after G–d has promised success. Adversity that seems to contradict G–d's will and His promises of blessing and reward leaves human beings frustrated, disappointed, and doubting. Abraham's faith is not eas-ily transferable to his descendants. Moses will have to forge his own revitalized belief in G–d from the fire of his own experiences and his generation's problems. The lesson of the conversation be-tween G–d and Moses is that faith, like Torah knowledge itself, is not inherited. It is earned anew in each generation.

Parents often question why children raised in a house of be-lief and observance can stray from the value system of Torah Judaism. Such a question should never be posed, for it erro-neously presupposes an automatic transfer of faith and belief from one generation to the next. Faith is not genetic. Faith comes from the depths of one's being, from the failures and dis-appointments of life, from the unanswerable paradoxes that fill our days, from the residue of resolve within us that daily life has not as yet chipped away. Faith has to be nurtured and en-hanced, discussed and debated, inspected and cleansed. All of the hard questions of life, the how's and the why's, the maybe's and should-be's, have to be resolutely faced, even if they can-not be answered with satisfaction. The sterling quality of our forefathers, in fact of all Jewish generations of the past, was the ability to bear enormous burdens of the soul and to construct from them construct a tower of faith for their times. By the end of Moses' life of leadership, 40 years after his complaint to G–d that his mission to Pharaoh was not working out, Moses would become the man of faith for his people. But that faith would first need to be hardened in the fires of dissension, in the disappointments and defeats of the desert, in the hurt of failed hopes and dashed dreams. Only out of such experiences does true faith assert itself and bring soothing balm to the aches of life.

Our Jewish generation has suffered more than its share of disappointments. After the survival of the Holocaust and the creation of the State of Israel, many felt that at least there would be no more disappointments and doubts. Our redemption was guaranteed, and it would take place now, we were assured. It hasn't quite happened that way yet. Like our teacher Moses, we will also have to continue to earn our faith — slowly, painfully, but surely.

Elijah, Angels, Strangers, Messengers

Joseph is sent by his father Jacob to visit his brothers, who are tending the family's sheep in the open pasture. Joseph is well aware of his brothers' enmity towards him. He is now also aware that his own words and actions may have contributed to their negative attitude. He therefore resolves that he will use the opportunity to visit his brothers to make amends with them. He is unaware of how desperate the situation truly is and how deeply his brothers fear him, seeing him as a threat to their very existence. He enters the zone of danger completely unprepared for what awaits him there.

And here the Divine hand intervenes. Joseph cannot find his brothers, who are not at their usual place of pasture. He is ready to return home, his father's mission and his own secret goal un-fulfilled. And suddenly, a stranger finds Joseph, lost and confused in the field. He tells him where he can locate his broth-ers, and Joseph, now with a light and confident step, sets out on his most fateful rendezvous. Because of the intervention of this unknown stranger, the rest of the famous story is allowed to unfold. The sale of Joseph, the 22-year separation from Jacob, his torturous Egyptian drama and triumph culminating in the fi-nal reuniting and reconciliation of the family of Israel, all would not have occurred without the appearance and seemingly in-nocuous instructions of this stranger. Who was he?

Rashi states that the stranger was the angel Gabriel, sent from heaven by G–d Himself to influence the course of events. Thus, Rashi sees this part of the story in purely supernatural terms. However, Ramban, in his commentary on these events, sees in the appearance of the stranger a natural validation of the princi-ple of Jewish belief that "man proposes and G–d disposes." "For the   prepared for him [Joseph] a [human] guide, unbeknownst to him, in order to lead Joseph into the hands [of his brothers]. This is to teach us that that man's diligence is unavailing, and only G–d's decree is valid. This is the teaching of our Rabbis that the stranger was an 'angel,' meaning that [he was fulfilling G–d's mission], and it is G–d's decrees that are always realized." Ram-ban teaches us that all of the "chance" occurrences that life brings to us, all of the strangers we may encounter, are to be viewed as G–d's "angels," seen in the perspective of our relation-ship to our Creator. A personal G–d is the G–d of Israel.

The advent of modernity two centuries ago pretty much did away with the concept of a personal G–d for much of Western civ-ilization. This sad denial of heavenly interest eventually invaded the Jewish world as well. Man became the sole arbiter of his fate, and it was believed that societies could become fine tuned to per-fection by adherence to new and progressive social theories. G–d no longer played a major role in human affairs. But now, at the end of the bloodiest century in human history, we are no longer so sanguine about our future. Empty of belief, frightened of ourselves, we recoil at meeting "strangers" and having to somehow rethink our lives in light of G–d's "angels," who constantly intrude upon our pursuit of our goals. The wise person looks for Divine aid in every occurrence and meeting of life. Judaism believes in the personal G–d of Israel Who guides and directs us. We should be alert to the next "stranger" or "angel" that we meet.

Maybe I Am Wrong!

The Torah informs us at length of the offerings contributed by the princes of the tribes of Israel at the inauguration of the *Mishkan*, the Tabernacle built by Bezalel in the desert of Sinai. Each of the princes is mentioned by name, and even though their offerings were identical, each offering is detailed separately in the Torah. Many insights as to the reason for this lengthy description have been advanced, though, as in many other matters of the spirit, the question may be stronger than the answers. Whatever the reason may be, there is a strong lesson that may be derived from the recounting of the offerings, and it is a matter of prime importance in our time of Jewish angst.

Of the 12 princes of Israel, two were the heads of the tribes of Manasseh and Ephraim, the descendants of Joseph. Jacob's blessing to Joseph was the twofold inheritance of the *bechor*, the firstborn. Manasseh and Ephraim became as Reuben and Simeon and were two of the 12 tribes of Israel after Levi was chosen for special service. Thus, all of Israel was constantly reminded that Joseph's dreams were realized and that he, and not his brothers, had the correct view of the Jewish future. When the princes of Manasseh and Ephraim entered the *Mishkan* and publicly made their offerings in front of G–d and Israel, all of the Jews had to acknowledge Joseph's worth.

What makes this important to us is the fact that Joseph's brothers were sincerely convinced that he had to be eliminated from their midst for the sake of Jewish survival! The 10 brothers acted against him in concert, convinced that they were doing a holy and noble deed by removing an enemy, if not a traitor, from their midst. Even when witnessing their father's never-ending grief and pain over the loss of his most beloved son, the brothers never wavered in their belief that they had done the right thing, the necessary thing, the moral and holy act. For people, even great people, sometimes err, feeling that erroneous means can somehow advance the cause of righteous goals. Unfortunately, we are witness to this type of behavior throughout the Jewish world, behavior whose results are always very unfortunate; the Rabin tragedy is the most extreme example of this self-assured but absurd act of violence. The appearance of the two representatives of Joseph in the holy *Mishkan*, centuries after Joseph had apparently been judged guilty by his brothers, was a Divine sign that human faith in the absolute correctness of a policy or action can be dangerous.

History has taught Jews that smugness, self-righteousness, and close-mindedness lead to disaster. A healthy measure of self-doubt and introspection about motives, policies, and behavior is in itself a holy trait. "Maybe *I* am the one who is wrong" is a thought that should always cross our minds and temper our speech and behavior. And we cannot employ non-Torah behavior in order to achieve Torah goals. Righteousness is advanced only through righteous means. The narrative describing the princes of Manasseh and Ephraim and their public offerings in the *Mishkan* serves as an annual reminder to us of these basic truths. It is an important lesson for us to remember in our assessment of personal and communal situations. Cautious and measured behavior is the key to all success in life.

IX
MODERN
CONCEPTS

The Right
Not to Know

There are many times in life when one is aware of a difficult personal situation that others are enduring. Suddenly, we may notice that the problem has somehow been resolved, and we notice the lifting of a great burden in the countenances of those others. Even though we may have been curious as to the nature of the problem and perhaps even more curious about its resolution, good manners prevent us from prying into the lives of others. So we rejoice in their relief and remain silent. However, there are instances in life when we are aware of others' problems and we do *not* wish to know more about it. We do not want to know the awful details of the problem. We are just happy that somehow it is all over, and we are satisfied to leave it at that. For the knowledge of that situation, we instinctively know, would prove painful to us as well.

The children of Jacob never tell him directly the details of Joseph's disappearance. They show him the bloody shirt and allow him to draw his own conclusions. They know that those conclusions are incorrect but, because of their personal involvement, they are powerless to correct Jacob's belief that his beloved Joseph is dead. How can they tell their father that they have sold their own brother as a slave? And that this was a way of commuting the death sentence that they had passed against him? The first seeds of doubt in the minds of the brothers about their behavior towards Joseph arose at that first heart-wrenching moment when they had to confront their father. Jacob does not ask them for details of the bloody shirt. They take an oath among themselves never to tell their father the awful truth. Long decades of painful, awkward silence and grief dominate the holy family of Israel. Jacob does not want to know. The brothers do not wish to tell.

And now it all ends suddenly and happily. Joseph lives and is the viceroy of Egypt. The family is moving to Egypt to be with Joseph. Jacob never asks Joseph or his brothers what really happened on that fateful day 22 years earlier. He is satisfied with the results and prefers not to delve into the details of the process. Yet on his deathbed he confides to Joseph, "I know, my son, I know." The entire story has been revealed to him intuitively, Divinely. There are times in life when it is better not to know, and even if one knows, not to raise the matter till he is on his deathbed.

Our society suffers from a surfeit of knowing. Thus, we have no heroes, no trusted leaders, no privacy in life because there is some mysterious "right to know" which dominates all else. In our times, acts and revelations which in previous generations would have been condemned as treasonous and dangerous to national welfare are cheered as being the fulfillment of the "right to know." Not everything need be known. Not everything known need be publicized and acted upon. There is great value in not prying, in not knowing everything, in patience, and in reticence. These are the qualities which allow Jacob to reunite his family after the debacle of Joseph's sale. He who comes to heal must always be committed not to harm. Jacob's extraordinary behavior regarding Joseph and his brothers illustrates this point clearly.

Old Receipts

Not long ago, I purchased an item at an exclusive shop as a wedding gift for a friend's child. Foolishly believing in the infallibility of my good taste, I neglected to keep the receipt for my purchase, though the box, the shopping bag, and the item itself all testified to its having been purchased from that store. The recipients of the gift (inexplicably) did not like it and attempted to return it to the store for exchange or refund. The store demanded that they produce the receipt. They asked me for it. I no longer had it. Our relationship became strained and uncomfortable, and I am certain that every time they see this unwanted and unappreciated gift of mine, they have very ambivalent feelings about it and about me. Why did I throw away that receipt? Because at that moment, it never dawned on me that it could turn into something important. I threw it away because at that moment it was not necessary to me. But a wise person sees ahead and realizes that items currently considered expendable may in the future be vitally necessary. That is part of the message of the Bible and Talmud, "A wise man has eyes in his head — he therefore sees what the future may bring."

In the struggle between the twin brothers, Jacob and Esau, the truth of this observation is validated. Esau, young, at the height of his physical powers, the champion hunter of the ancient world, scorns the spiritual birthright that was his inheritance from his father, Isaac, and his grandfather, Abraham. In his own words, "What do I need a birthright for?" So he throws away the unnecessary receipt, seeing it only as a useless scrap of paper. "And Esau demeaned the birthright in his eyes." To him it is of no value. He is handsome, attractive, strong, wealthy. He has friends who fawn over him, leisure and good times that await him. Therefore, his birthright, his tradition, his heritage, are a burden to him — archaic, outmoded, and unwanted. But Esau will grow older and less certain of his prowess and his future. New champions are arising to dethrone him, his wealth has become more precarious, and he now sees the terribly uncertain future, even the grave, staring at him. He can no longer live a life in the present. In panic, he returns to his aged, blind, but far-seeing father and begs for the return of his birthright, for the blessing of his family's heritage and tradition. But once the receipt is discarded, it is difficult, sometimes impossible, to retrieve it.

In the optimistic and naive blush of enlightened youth that has characterized the last two centuries of Western civilization, society — both general and Jewish — has discarded the moral birthright that had taken millennia to develop. And now, at the end of the bloodiest century in human history, the collapse of all the theories and "isms" of modern man is apparent. We would like to restore our original birthright, but the road is long, complex, and strewn with mines. It is extremely difficult to rebuild a Jewish home, a Jewish family, a Jewish way of life, after generations of denigration and neglect of Torah values. But we have no choice but to attempt to find our way home. And we should also realize by now that in our exuberance for the present, we should be wise and disciplined enough not to discard the past cavalierly. We may yet sorely need that receipt.

Preconceptions and Disaster

Though Balaam is undoubtedly the main villain and most intriguing character in the Torah's drama of the attempt to curse Israel, the auxiliary character in the story, Balak, king of Moab, also deserves our attention. Balak is an inscrutable figure. He was aware of the fact that the people of Israel were restrained by Divine fiat from attacking Moab. Moab was still protected from attack by the Jews by virtue of being descended from Lot, the nephew of Abraham. Logic would dictate that Balak assume a passive and neutral posture toward the people of Israel and not go out of his way to provoke a potentially powerful foe that is currently committed to peaceful relations with him and his kingdom. But history and the study of human behavior teaches us that people, even kings and leaders, do not behave logically, nor do they necessarily behave in their own interest. Therefore, Balak has to be viewed not as a wise and discerning leader, but rather as an ordinary mortal, subject to terrible personal prejudices, misjudgments, and short-sightedness. Balaam is greedy, and that terrible corruption is what leads to his disastrous behavior. Balak is small and petty, bigoted and stubborn, and his ingrained attitudes force him into nationally suicidal behavior.

There are many such examples in our century of the failure of leaders to behave wisely. Hitler's preconceived notions of Slavic subhumanity, Bolshevik inefficiency, and Jewish dominance of Stalin's Russia all combined to lead him into the fatal error of invading Russia — a Russia that desperately desired the continuance of its nonaggression treaty with Germany. There were no doubts in Hitler's mind that he assessed the situation correctly. Any objective observer would have been wary of a war with Russia, considering its enormous population and territory. But wisdom is never present when prejudice and self-righteousness rule. Balak is so convinced of the evil intentions and hatred of Israel that he commits national suicide, first by inviting Balaam to curse it and then by convincing Moab and Sihon to war against Israel, when there is absolutely no real danger to him or his kingdom. The Rabbis liken his behavior to one who provokes and enrages a wild dog when it is obvious that the dog has already passed him by. But such is the behavior of those with small minds, stubbornly held preconceptions, and deep-seated, irrational prejudices. Unfortunately, when these traits exist in a leader, millions suffer. We have a lot to learn from Balak's failures!

The contemporary Jewish community could also benefit from a more objective approach to its problems and challenges. People in high places in Jewish life are convinced that American Jews are unwilling to commit themselves to a more observant, Torah-oriented life-style, even though all agree that it is the surest (if not the only) solution to the problem of rampant Jewish assimilation in America. In a recent article in *The Wall Street Journal*, Dennis Prager wrote that the solution for American Jewry is to emulate Orthodox Jews. "The Orthodox keep their children Jewish, and they possess a defining characteristic of religious people — tension with the dominant culture. The only Jewish movement resisting secular liberalism is Orthodoxy." But Prager then dismisses this logic by stating "that there is no reason to assume that most Jews will ever become Orthodox." Therefore, what? Is this not another case of a prejudgment, like Balak's, that always lead to disaster? I think that Jews who want to remain Jewish will become more observant. It is this logic that will eventually prevail.

Diversity
and Transition

The death of Jacob marks the end of the Era of the *Avos* — the great Patriarchs of Israel. No longer will the story of G–d's revelation to man deal only with individuals, or at most with a nuclear family, but it will now encompass a relationship with an entire nation. The story of Israel will now take on a much broader dimension, infinitely more complex and problematic, and deciphering it will require much greater vision. But Jacob's children will have to pass through a period of transition between family and nationhood. Such passages in human history are always difficult and not always successfully negotiated. In order to insure that the period of transition will not destroy the nascent nation of Israel, Jacob gives individual, personal blessings to his children to guide them. In his words of benediction, he combines their personal qualities and achievements with their future national aspirations. This far-seeing approach will enable the Jewish people to bridge the chasm between the Era of the *Avos* — the Patriarchs — and the great challenge of the birth of nationhood.

Our century has been witness to the awful demands of nationhood upon individuals. All of the bloody, totalitarian regimes of our time (Hitler's Germany, Stalin's Russia, Amin's Uganda, Mao's China, Tojo's Japan, Hussein's Iraq, Nasser's Egypt, to name only a few) have distinguished themselves in the obliteration of the individuality of their citizens. Big Brother knows best. Everyone dresses alike, thinks alike, behaves alike, and is subservient to the demands of the nation. What a recipe for human disaster! For it is only in a society that allows the individual to retain his uniqueness, to contribute from his talents and singularity, that a strong loyalty to nationhood can be developed. Jacob recognizes this; he emphasizes first the distinctive qualities of each of his sons, and then he blesses them with the challenge of unity and nationhood. By impressing upon them the need for individuality in the time of nation-building, Jacob assures that the painful period of transition from family to nation will be a success.

The Jewish people in our time are also passing through a difficult transition, from millennia of exile to an era of uncertain national independence. It is one thing to dream of an imaginary Jerusalem of spirit and holiness. It is quite another challenge to deal with an urban mass of land and people, an earthly, crowded, noisy, and diverse Jerusalem, and to make it productive and harmonious. The temptation to regulate and control, to make individuals completely subservient to the perceived national interest is tempting, perhaps even comforting. But our father Jacob, through his example, has taught us that it would be self-defeating to follow such a policy. Each of the tribes of Israel, every individual Jew, has a unique contribution to make to the matrix of Israel. Everyone united does not mean everyone the same. Remembering that the diversity of Jews is an asset and not a liability will help us through this difficult era of transition. The Torah that teaches us that human beings are innately diverse also unites us in our goals and dreams. That is Jacob's blessing to us all, his loving and loyal descendants.

Light and Darkness

Human beings are afraid of darkness. From our infancy and childhood on, we are always interested in having some sort of night light, physical or imaginary, burning. Before the advent of gas and electric street-lighting, people locked themselves in their homes at night and waited for the comfort of day before venturing out again. For darkness is a fearsome foe of man's well-being and of a balanced psyche. What we cannot make out clearly is much more frightening than clearly delineated threats. All of our pains and frights, apprehensions and anxieties, doubts and uncertainties are magnified in darkness. To put it succinctly, darkness is depressing!

One of the 10 plagues visited upon Egypt, preparatory to the Jewish exodus from that house of bondage, was darkness — a palpable, paralyzing, horrendous darkness. It allowed for no human activity or movement. It broke the will and spirit of the people of Egypt, though Pharaoh would still hang on for one more blow before succumbing. What made the plague of darkness even more devastating to the Egyptians was the realization that "for all of the children of Israel there was light in their dwellings." Universal blackouts are always more acceptable than selective ones. If one's entire neighborhood suffers a power failure, he can usually take the matter in stride. If, however, his neighbor has lights on while he has to sit in darkness, then the frustration of life's unfairness begins to boil over.

I have always felt that one of the causes for the world's unceasing hatred of the Jew over the centuries was the fact that Jews apparently had their lights on while much of the rest of civilization was bathed in darkness. Europe was in the Dark Ages while the Jews were in the period of the Talmud, the *Geonim*, and the early *Rishonim*. As a famous Israeli diplomat was wont to remind his colleagues in the U.N., "Jerusalem was the spiritual capital of the world when London and Paris were still mere swamps." The Jew felt a pride that the lights were always on in his home. He attempted to focus his light of morality, civilized values, probity of speech, behavior, and values on his surrounding neighbors as well, but he was never ready to equalize the blackout, to invite darkness into his own home and heart. As such, he was resented by his neighbors, but he was also envied by them. They attempted, therefore, to extinguish the light of the Jewish home, if not the Jew himself, in order to make everyone the same. But the world has never succeeded in extinguishing the Jewish light.

However, the past centuries of Enlightenment, secularism, nationalism, and above all, abysmal ignorance of Judaism, have allowed much darkness to penetrate our Jewish camp. No longer do we feel ourselves to be "a light unto the nations." We are now paralyzed by the fears engendered by the sudden invasion of darkness in our homes and families. We have become like our neighbors, and our house is as dark as theirs. But we still have a generator that can power our homes and fill them with light. This magical generator is our sense of spirituality and eternity that the Torah has outlined for us. By attaching ourselves to it, we will guarantee that "for all of the children of Israel there will be light in their dwellings."

Winning by "Losing"

There are a number of violent and potentially violent scenes in the story of our father Jacob. Jacob's confrontation with his vengeful brother, Esau; the kidnapping and assault of Dinah, Jacob's daughter; the subsequent sacking of the city of Shechem by Simeon and Levi; and the wars of Jacob's family with the surrounding tribes attempting to avenge Shechem and prevent Jacob's return to Hebron and Beersheba — all of these are very discomforting experiences in the life of our great patriarch. It is therefore interesting to note that in each of these crisis situations

Jacob adopts a low-profile, nonviolent, even somewhat accommodating stance. While Simeon and Levi heroically proclaim their policy of avenging their sister's shame in blood, their father Jacob remains silently disapproving, not wishing to debate the matter with them further. This is in keeping with Jacob's general philosophy, for when the angel of Esau was within his grasp and begging for release, Jacob loosened his hold upon him and limped away himself, preferring the nonviolent moral victory to the actual triumph of arms and strength.

I do not mean to advocate pacifism at all costs as a Torah value or Jewish virtue. Self-defense, strength of arms along with a willingness to use them when necessary, and a perception of power are all essential and admired attributes in a dangerous world. The Jewish historical experience is replete with examples of military bravery and success. We are certainly aware that the State of Israel has been engaged in an unremitting war for the last half-century, and without power and violent deterrent strength its very existence would be jeopardized. And yet after all of this has been said, it is abundantly clear that violence is a tactic and never a solution. The ultimate victory is never secured by force of arms alone. The map of Europe has been redrawn regularly over the past millennia without solving the basic problems of its contentious populations. The symbol of Chanukah, chosen by the wise men of Israel to commemorate the Hasmonean victory over the Syrian Greeks, is not the sword and shield of Jewish arms, but rather the spiritual light of the holy menorah. The words of the prophet Zechariah symbolize the futility of applying violent solutions to complex human problems: "Not by power nor by strength, but rather by My spirit, says the L–rd of Hosts." This is the confirmation of the way of Jacob. It is the long-standing tradition of Judaism regarding human affairs.

Jacob knows that he will meet his brother Esau again and again in their intersecting journeys through history. Jacob is confident that at the end of time, "saviors will climb Mount Zion and judge Mount Esau." But that will not necessarily be a violent moment of confrontation, for the result of that judgment will be that "all sovereignty on earth will belong to G–d." That is Jacob's goal: not might or power or dominion, but understanding, truth, and service of the Creator. Even if we are forced by others to be warriors, we should realize that our ultimate triumph lies in the realm of the spirit and in the fulfillment of our G–d-given mission of Torah and goodness in every facet of our lives.

The Rule of the Majority

Is the majority always right? Well, we all know enough history to realize that the answer to that question is a resounding "no." The majority can be as tyrannical and error-prone as any dictator or political megalomaniac. Some of the worst leaders in modern history were elected by healthy majorities in democratically held elections. Terribly fateful and ultimately tragic decisions were approved by the popular will of the time. The truth is that following the will of the majority is no guarantee of wise policies. Current wisdom is always fleeting, circumstances change, and the majority decision may be fashionable but not always healthy. Winston Churchill assessed democracy as "being a terribly inefficient and problematic way of governing, but it is far better than any other system ever tried," and the idea of majority rule has certainly struck deep roots in our society. But one of the main problems of our system is how to protect the minority. A failure to do so has always resulted in strife, tension, and civil war.

The Torah states: "You shall not follow the majority *l'raos.*" What does that Hebrew word mean? Many translate it as "doing evil" or following the majority of the court (the Talmud construes the verse narrowly to apply mainly to court cases and judges' deliberations) or society in perpetrating something which is wrong, even if it is popular. But others think that the implication here is not one of actual evil *behavior* on the part of the majority, since the Torah has already cautioned us against this in all of its previous teachings, continually stressing the importance of not falling victim to the trap of evil conduct "because everyone is doing it"! Rather, the Torah is emphasizing the establishment of those *standards* of right and wrong that will not be subject to majority rule and changing societal circumstances.

Moral behavior requires moral standards, a simple fact which has unfortunately been overlooked in modern social science. That is why the Torah reading about majority rule follows the Torah reading containing the Ten Commandments. Societies change, technology advances, governments, economic systems, and social theories rise and fall; nothing in life remains static. But the basic moral code of defining right and wrong must remain unchangeable, for otherwise the meaning of the concepts "right" and "wrong" is nonexistent. We have to follow the majority in many facets of human life. The Torah itself dictates "After the opinion of the many shall you decide judgments." But legal judgments, statistical probabilities, governmental elections, all of which follow the rule of the majority, are not moral standards per se (though they may eventually force an individual to make moral choices). In matters of morals, the majority does not change the godly definitions of moral standards.

For the Person Who Has Everything

One of the great questions in life is, "What can you give to someone who has everything?" The truth is that there are very few people in life who feel that they have everything. There are even fewer whose self-satisfaction is so great that it is apparent to others. In the great museums of Russia, one may today see the fabulous Fabergé "eggs" — made of gold and encrusted with diamonds, pearls, and other precious stones, all in magnificent settings — that were created as gifts from the czars to their czarinas, who seemingly had "everything." But they didn't have those "eggs"! And in retrospect, the czars and czarinas of Russia didn't have that much of "everything," as their history, family problems, and violent deaths proved. I have often remarked that the Torah represents Esau as having "a great deal" — "*yesh li rav*" — and Jacob as having "everything" — "*yesh li kol.*" In traditional Jewish thought, this difference between "*kol,*" everything, and "*rav,*" a great deal, is the sign of Jacob's moral superiority over Esau. But if Jacob has "everything," why does this not register upon Esau and thereby influence his way of life? I have long been troubled by the fact that if the Torah way of life is so authentic and spiritual — which it is — and if the serenity and restorative peace of the Sabbath is so palatable — which it is — then where are all of those otherwise wonderful Jews when it comes to matters of observance and a Jewish way of life?

The obvious answer is that one may somehow internally achieve the blessing of having "everything," but that fact is not apparent to others. There can be many reasons for this paradox. One contributing factor may be a lack of openness and communication on both parts. In fact, the person who has "everything" (in a spiritual and emotional sense) is hardly likely to advertise the fact, for such an attitude borders on spiteful insensitivity, which is not in accordance with the Torah view of having "everything." Thus, this cautious reticence about having "everything," by its very nature, keeps others from seeing the contentment.

Another factor contributing to the lack of enthusiasm to have "everything" is seen in the eternal conundrum of why G–d allows the wicked to prosper and the good to be smitten. It may very well be that Jacob has everything and Esau only has a great deal, but that is not quite how it appears to Esau and to the rest of the world. Jacob is alone, while Esau is popular. Jacob is burdened, attacked, and persecuted, while Esau is strong, respected, and well established. Jacob limps and apologizes, while Esau struts and issues definitive orders. The world, understandably but short-sightedly, prefers Esau's "great deal" to Jacob's "everything." Therefore, Jacob's way is never an openly attractive one. Nevertheless, wise people see life in the long range and not just for its temporary satisfaction. Their definition of "everything" carries spiritual and moral thrust and is not measured solely by material criteria.

One of the hallmarks of Jewish tradition has been its assurance that living a moral, observant Torah way of life, serving G–d and man and tending to one's soul, is the way to really have "everything." In a world that foolishly and single-mindedly pursues financial and social one-upmanship, where it sometimes seems that nothing is ever enough and "everything" is an elusive goal, it is essential that we reestablish within our lives the priorities of Jacob, a satisfaction with our share in life, an appreciation of health, years, family, spiritual growth, our glorious history and tradition, and a sense of fulfillment in striving to be a holy people.

Freedom
and Liberty

The famous Liberty Bell, the symbol of the American Revolution located in Philadelphia, has inscribed upon it a Biblical verse taken from the Torah: "Proclaim liberty unto the land and to all its inhabitants." The verse itself, in the context of the subject matter in that chapter of the Bible, can be construed narrowly to mean that the land is "freed" from the ownership of the purchaser and returned to the original owner every Jubilee year. Thus, the appropriation of that verse to justify the political purposes of the American Revolution may appear somewhat questionable. Yet, upon deeper analysis of the verse and the g–dly purpose behind the holy words of the Torah, there is justification for viewing the verse in a broader aspect rather than for its literal definition alone. Proclaiming liberty is a Torah imperative that applies to all individuals, nations, times, and circumstances. There is no substitute for individual liberty, for it alone justifies the possibility of freedom of will and choice, and the resultant reward and punishment philosophy of Judaism. The Torah teaches us that only a free person can truly serve G–d, and this is the meaning of the Rabbis' statement that only one who is involved in Torah is truly a free person.

Possessions have a tendency to enslave us. The Torah bids us to "give freedom to the land," meaning not only to free land for return to its original owner, but to give *ourselves* freedom *from* that land, from the binding chains of materialism that often force disastrous choices upon us. Once we feel that we own something, that we have earned it, that somehow it is ours, we find it almost impossible to part with it, often to our own detriment. A proper view of the place of possessions in our lives is one of the primary goals of a Torah perspective. Judaism never preaches poverty per se as a virtue, and property certainly plays an important role in human life. Nevertheless, it is obvious that humans should possess goods and not vice versa. Freedom from the slavery and dominance of possessions is a necessity for one to live a life of true holiness.

The entire concept of the Jubilee year — *Yovel* — is one of freedom and rebirth. The great slogan of the late Chief Rabbi Avraham Yitzchak Kook, was "to renew and revitalize the old, and to sanctify the new." Our task is not to discard the old, to cast off traditional Jewish values and mores, but rather to infuse them with a new sense of enthusiasm and purpose, and — to paraphrase Lincoln — to give them a new birth of freedom. But the sense of freedom that is required is not solely an external loosening of the bonds of oppression; rather, in our times, it is also a strong sense of internal liberty and happiness, the feeling of being in control of our lives and possessions rather than being controlled by them. So let us listen to our own internal Liberty Bell and "proclaim liberty unto the land and all its inhabitants."

Confusing Jews with Judaism

Human reaction to Divine commandments has always been varied. It ranges from the extremes of almost blind obedience and acceptance to open defiance and rebellion. The power of free will — the ultimate gift of G–d to His creatures — allows for an infinite number of behavioral responses to the commandments of the Creator. But human responses change and adjust over time, so that our reaction to faith and to Torah is never static, but rather constantly evolving. We become either more g–dly, so to speak, or more self-centered and earth bound; but we never remain the same, spiritually speaking, for any extended period of time.

The Torah describes an incident of strife and blasphemy that occurred in the camp of Israel during the sojourn of the Jews in the Sinai desert. A man, born of a non-Jewish father and a Jewish mother, fought with another Jew. This man objected to the treatment that he allegedly suffered when he was refused membership in the tribe of Dan and prevented from pitching his tent in that tribe's camp. The Torah law is that, even though the question of one's Jewishness is decided exclusively by matrilineal descent, the decision as to the tribal identification of any individual Jew — such as being a *kohen* or a *levi* — is a matter of patrilineal descent. Having an Egyptian father automatically disqualified this man from membership in the tribe of Dan, his mother's tribe. When he refused to accept this Torah law and attempted to force his way into the tribe's camp, a man from Dan tried to prevent him physically from doing so. The ensuing fight caused a furor. The interloper finally vented his contempt for the Torah of Israel and its Author by blaspheming the Name of G–d itself. His original hurt, personal though it was, flared and developed into a rejection of Torah, and finally into an act of reviling G–d Himself.

This is the unfortunate pattern that has marked much of modern Jewish secularist life. People felt personally hurt by alleged wrongs that they attributed to the Torah of Israel or its supposed representatives. They felt justified in rejecting Torah commandments, Torah values, and the traditions of Israel on the basis that they were restrictive and irrelevant to the brave new world of the 20th century; but they still felt *Jewish* and were part of the Jewish nation and destiny.

The matter, however, rapidly deteriorated. They and their descendants soon attempted to force themselves on the traditional camp of Israel, trying to impose new, non-Torah standards on the ancient ways of Jewish life. And when their attempts to re-define Torah and Judaism were resisted by other Jews, they fought with those Jews, mocking and reviling them. This led to the next stage of rebellion, which was marked by a complete re-jection of Torah and its centrality in Jewish life. Finally, the rebellion sank into an exercise of atheism, blasphemy, and Jew-ish self-hatred. Today, as a result of this two-centuries-old process, a large percentage of the Jewish people not only do not behave Jewishly, but no longer feel or identify themselves as *Jewish*. This must be seen as tantamount to spiritual suicide and national disaster. How tragic for the story of this young blasphemer to be repeated in such numbers in front of our eyes.

But the tide is reversing. The Torah is taking a more central place in Jewish life again. There are more Jews who wish to be-lieve rather than to blaspheme. Let us encourage this trend and bless the G–d and destiny of Israel by our behavior, attitudes, and words.

Competition

Competition is an accepted condition in our society. In commerce, sports, government, the arts and sci-ences, competition is the fuel for the engine that drives our society forward. Without competition we would be at the mercy of monopolists, cartels, and a controlled society that would stifle all progress or incentive for personal reward. The Talmud itself speaks highly of competi-tion, at least in educational and scholarly matters, when it states that "competition amongst scholars increases wisdom and knowledge." Nevertheless, like all positive attributes, competi-tion should have its limits. Unrestrained, cutthroat, vicious competition is immoral and eventually counterproductive. The

Torah reading of *Shoftim* introduces the prohibition against the concept of *"hasagat g'vul"* — unfair competition. The Hebrew phrase *hasagat g'vul* literally mean overstepping or illegally encroaching on a neighbor's border. Just as it is wrong to move one's fence to gobble up a piece of the neighboring lot, so too is it wrong to engage in unfair competitive practices, injuring someone else's business to benefit one's own. As naive and altruistic as this view may appear at first glance, there is sound social and economic sense behind it.

The Torah is interested in creating a fair, just, harmonious, and compassionate society. Unfair competition, when practiced openly and without shame, prevents the development of such a society. In the words of Rabbi Abraham ibn Ezra, the great philosopher, poet, and Biblical commentator of the 12th century, "Unfair competition [such as border encroachment] automatically leads to quarrels, violence, and even murder." Rapacious economic practices in the 18th and 19th centuries led to the reactions of socialism, Communism, and other state-controlled economies in the 20th century. The prophecy of ibn Ezra of "quarrels, violence, and even murder" was thus fulfilled in front of our horrified eyes. Excess begets excess, and greedy, exploitative competition begets state-controlled, repressive monopoly and tyranny.

Thus, the Torah frowns on negative remarks about competitors' products and personalities. Negative advertising, whether in politics, commercial services, or manufactured products, is not allowed and is considered a definite form of *lashon harah,* evil speech. One may describe accurately and even boast about the wonderful qualities of his own products or services, but it is unfair competition to knock those of the other person. I know that this sounds strange to 20th-century American consumers, who are bombarded by telemarketing, incessant advertising, and a terribly negative promotional atmosphere. But Jews and their understanding of life have always been bidden to swim upstream against the current.

I think that the prohibition against "encroaching on the border" applies to many areas of life. Following this precept guarantees the sanctity of privacy, the holiness of confidentiality, and the civility necessary for a fair and trustworthy marketplace. Even in family life there is considerable competition for time, attention, and love; in fact, it is probably within the family circle, at the very beginnings of social life itself, that the lessons of proper competition should be taught and learned. Respect for righteous norms, the understanding of the Divine imperative to allow for others' success, and respect for the basic Jewish idea that no one really takes from anyone else are all together the substance of Torah life. No "encroachment on the border" should be part of our outlook.

Hearing

The Hebrew word "*haazinu*," in its literal sense, is a command to hear — or better, to listen. It is the Biblical equivalent of Shakespeare's "lend me your ears." The immediate object of this command in Moses' final words to Israel are the heavens and the earth, as the verse indicates. But certainly, in a deeper sense, the true target of Moses' request and demand for attention are the ears of the Jewish people. It is noteworthy that the Torah places strong emphasis on our physical senses. Earlier in the book of *Devarim*, Moses challenged the Jewish people by saying, "*Re'eh* — see!" Now he challenges them to "hear." The great King David, in one of his psalms, demands that Israel "taste and see the goodness of G–d!" In the Torah's description of the plague of darkness that befell the Egyptians before the Jewish exodus, the phrase used is that "the darkness was to be felt." All of this is meant to convey to us that service of G–d and spiritual growth are not limited to the realm of the imagination and the soul alone. True spirituality is a product of the physical senses — the ability to hear and see, to taste and feel.

But in order for the senses to lead to greater spiritual growth, one must develop them so that they are keen and sensitive. There is much in life that we hear, but little that we truly listen to. From our spouse's banter and conversation, to the background noises of the house and the street, and even (or perhaps especially) to the sermon of the rabbi, we are able to hear but not listen. The phrase "to tune out" has become a stock idiom in describing our lives and attitudes. But if we would be able to truly listen, to follow Moses' demand of "*haazinu*," then much more in life would be simpler and more satisfying for us. We are bidden to "tune out" gossip and slander, hateful and obscene words, and to listen instead to the "still, small voice" of G–d and tradition in our lives. Most of us at some point need corrective lenses in order to see well. The Torah, through practical observance of *mitzvos,* through a kosher kitchen and a *mezuzah* on our doorposts, through the sanctity of the Sabbath and the holidays, provides these "corrective lenses" for us so that we can see our way clearly through life's small print. We are to taste the sweetness of the Torah through its study, and we are to feel our way out of the oppressive darkness that surrounds us by firmly grasping the hands of those who preceded us.

The description in *Psalms* of idols and their worshipers is as follows: "They have eyes but see not, they have ears but hear not, nostrils but without breath, legs that do not walk!" Bereft of spiritual direction, physical senses, skills, and attributes sooner or later diminish and even atrophy. Nothing physical is eternal. However, physical qualities, when channeled toward the spiritual goals of Torah, acquire by osmosis an immortal character. We should renew our efforts to listen carefully, to see acutely, to feel keenly, and to taste discriminatingly the gifts and opportunities G–d has given us. The Torah of life that accompanies us continually on our earthly journey will help us develop our senses in order that we may truly be of service to G–d and man.

How to Remember

The Torah discusses the *mitzvah* of *tzitzis,* the wearing of the ritually prescribed eight-stringed "fringes" at the corners of a four-cornered garment, usually the *tallis* worn during prayer services in the synagogue. For many of the ritual commandments prescribed by the Torah, no explanation is ever advanced. It is simply a matter of pure faith that motivates Jews to observe that *mitzvah.* However, the Torah specifically explains to us the reason behind *tzitzis.* The "fringes" on the corners of our garments are meant to be a constant memory aid for Jews: "So that you shall remember and observe all the commandments that I have commanded you." The continuing reminder of our Divine obligations provided by *tzitzis* will help us be morally strong so that we "shall not be led astray, following the desires of our eyes and our hearts."

Tzitzis proved to be so important to Jewish life that Jews purposely wore an extra four-cornered garment — a *tallis katan* (small *tallis*) — as part of their daily dress, so that they would have the opportunity to fulfill this obligation constantly. The Talmud records instances when people about to commit mortal sins were saved from their own worst inclinations by the fact that the *tzitzis* they were wearing "rose to smite them in their eyes." Thus, *tzitzis* assumed a primary role — a tangible representation of G–d's presence in our lives.

I witnessed a powerful example of the influence of *tzitzis* on individual life over 20 years ago when I was the rabbinic administrator of the OU Kashruth Division. The OU was then working with a number of companies to try and develop a practical holding and slaughtering pen for calves and lambs to be used in kosher slaughterhouses in the United States. Such a pen already existed and was in wide use for steers, bulls, and cows, but there was no design yet available for the smaller animals such as calves and lambs. On a dismal rain-and-wind-swept day, I drove up to the University of Connecticut for an experimental demonstration of their latest proposed model for such a pen. Accompanying me was one of the leading *shochtim* (ritual kosher slaughterers) in America, who was going to participate in this demonstration. A survivor of Auschwitz, he was a handsome man with a great white beard and wise eyes always tinged by the tragedy he had experienced. A young Jewish researcher welcomed us and took us to a dressing room where we could change for the bloody task ahead.

The young man stared at the bearded *shochet* in amazement when, in the process of undressing, he removed his *tallis katan* with its attached *tzitzis*. "What is that?" he asked me in a whisper. In removing his shirt, the *shochet* had also revealed his bare arm, tattooed with his Auschwitz number. The young man asked me, a second question: "What are those numbers on his arm?" I responded that both the *tzitzis* and the tattoo were reminders of the faith and Judaism of the *shochet*. When the young man wanted to continue the conversation after the demonstration ended, I was hurried and really didn't give him the time he deserved. But I did give him the name of a young rabbi in his area who might help him.

A year later, long after I had forgotten the matter, the young man called me to tell me that he had been studying Judaism all year, that he was now on his way to Israel for another year's study of Torah, and that he was now wearing *tzitzis* regularly. And so the words of the Talmud that "*tzitzis* rise up and smite one in the eye" came true before my eyes.

Giving and Giving Again

The truth be said, it is difficult to open one's hand and give away money to the poor. There is an inherent feeling of resentment at being put upon because of the problems of others. Many times we feel exploited by the beggar who places his or her hand in front of us. Unanswered questions nag at us. Why is he/she begging? Is his/her tale of woe legitimate and true? Is there no other way that the problem can be solved except by begging? Why aren't the government and communal welfare agencies, to which I pay taxes and donate services and money, aware of this situation? And no matter what our final reaction to the outstretched hand is, no matter how much money we place in that hand, there is always a residual feeling of guilt that remains with us. Such encounters with the poor are almost always troubling and leave us with a wealth of ambivalent feelings.

The Torah gives us the cheerful news "that the poor will never become extinct from earthly society." This being the case, the admonition of the Torah that we are bidden to take care of the poor is always in place. "You shall not harden your heart, nor shall you shut your hand towards your brethren, the poor. Rather, you shall open your hand to him and surely provide him whatever he truly lacks." This is the law of the Torah, and it has been a definitive quality of Jewish life since the beginnings of our people, when our father Abraham set the pattern. The Talmud teaches us that the obligation to give to the poor is not a one-time requirement. It states that the Torah phrase "surely provide" indicates that one must continually provide for the poor — even the same poor person — "even 100 times." The Torah thus teaches us that compassion for our fellow man is a learned trait and should never be thought of as a mere sentiment. A learned trait requires practice and repetition. It is a skill to be cultivated and constantly honed. Therefore, we must train ourselves to give regularly, "even 100 times," for the act of constant giving itself is the training exercise, enabling us to avoid the gnawing doubts and feelings of guilt that are inevitably associated with charity and the poor.

One of the pillars of Jewish life, even of civilization at large, is compassion for others, a major form of which is charity. Jewish society has developed organized philanthropy to the level of an art form. But charity is measured not just by institutional size and by the amounts of money raised and distributed. The Torah measures it by one's personal response to the beggar who confronts him. It may be easier to write a large check to an organization than to give a small donation to a woefully poor person facing us. Thus, the Torah emphasizes the necessity of training for the proper giving of charity.

What's in a Name?

The narrative of Israel's sojourn in Egypt and its eventual redemption from the crushing physical and spiritual degradation of enslavement begins by telling us the names of the children of Jacob who came to Egypt during Joseph's reign. In fact, the entire second book of *Chumash,* as well as the first portion in that book, bears the title *Sh'mos* — "names." It is certainly an odd title for the story. For after all, "What's in a name?" Apparently the Torah is of the opinion that names are very important for Jewish identity and survival, both on a personal and national level. In fact, the Midrash teaches us that one of the strongest remaining commitments to holiness amongst the Jews in

Egypt, who were trapped in paganism, was that "they did not attempt to change their names."

So, in the eyes of Torah, names do matter. And in all of Jewish traditional life, names matter very deeply. There is somehow a feeling, mystical yet logical, that a person takes on the persona of the name he bears, even of the personality and traits of other Jews who bore that name before him. Names identify us, not only to the outside world, but even more importantly to ourselves. A name is what first gives a child a sense of uniqueness, of the special realization of difference so necessary for a healthy psyche. As an astute grandfather, I have noticed a few times amongst my grandchildren that acute sense of pain and confusion that comes when a child first discovers that someone else also has his or her name. Yes, names are special because we define ourselves through them. After a while, they cease being merely what we are called, but instead become our very essence.

A large number of Hebrew names contain the name of G–d within them. Jews wanted their children to sense from their earliest moments of cognitive understanding that humans have an ongoing, intimate, and eternal relationship with their Creator. Therefore, such names became the names of the royal family of David (*Yedidyah Shlomo, Amatzyah, Chizkayahu, Yoshiyahu, Zidkayahu,* etc.), the names of the prophets of Israel (*Yeshayahu, Yirmiyahu, Yechezkel, Ovadyahu, Zephanyah,* etc.), of the Hasmonean rulers (*Mattisyahu, Yochanan, Elazar, Yehonasan, Yochanan,* etc.) and of scores of Jewish children in later generations. Over the last two centuries, as the Jewish world in both the Diaspora and the Land of Israel became increasingly secularized and divorced from their traditional heritage, new names supplanted the old Biblical, G–d-oriented, Jewish historical names. Dror, Dorit, Eitan, Ronit, Ram, Ron, all became the fashion. I have no objection or criticism to the use of these names. I merely point out that they have no connection to the Jewish G–d, to Jewish heroes, to the Jewish past. I do not feel that they convey any sense of *Jewish* identity to the young who bear them. They are Israeli, in a very secular way, just as the "English" names we give our children in the Diaspora are English or American or French, in a very secular way. Again, no criticism is meant, just observation.

In a time when strong commitments to Jewish life are difficult to forge, fragile, and uncertain, remembering our true names and what they represent can be of good use to us. It helped us to achieve our redemption once before; it can help us achieve our ultimate redemption in the future.

The Quiet Revolution

I sense a quiet revolution taking place in American Jewry over the past few years. Though it has yet to translate itself into vast numbers of observant Jews, the search for Jewish identity is nevertheless gaining a momentum that may yet result in a much more committed and observant Jewish community. Wherever I travel in America, speaking to a wide variety of American Jews, I sense a more interested, searching, serious, albeit still somewhat skeptical, Jew. I also sense a search for a more spiritual, ethical, value-oriented life. This mood, brought about by many factors in Jewish and general society, can be a most positive development in Jewish life in this country, if it is properly exploited.

And, aye, that is the rub! For much of Orthodox Jewry, still hunkered down in the defensive posture forced upon it over the past decades of American Jewish life, does not seem prepared to deal with the situation realistically and positively. Nevertheless, there are quite a few imaginative programs that are successfully bringing Torah to those who thirst for it, programs such as SEED, Partners in Torah, Gateway, and Discovery.

In a spirited exchange of views that appeared in the November 1996 issue of *The Jewish Observer* on the subject of traditional Jewry's attitude towards the Reform and Conservative movements, Rabbi Elchonon Oberstein wrote as follows: "Agudath Israel has won the battle against pluralism. Orthodox rabbis under 65 who will sit on boards of rabbis are hard to find. Our own children are not in the least impressed with these [Conservative and Reform] movements, and they are not the slightest threat to 'Torah-true Judaism.' This was not the case a generation ago when Rabbi Aaron Kotler dramatically changed the way Orthodoxy dealt with heterodoxy. Now it is time to see what the reality is and reassess our approach.

"We know [that] what really works [to preserve Jewish continuity] is Torah and *mitzvos*. Yet, because we have chosen to legitimize Reform and Conservative rabbis by writing polemics and treating them as ideological adversaries, we have cut ourselves off from many opportunities to influence individuals and demonstrate what Orthodoxy really is ... [A] rabbi, widely admired as a great *talmid chacham,* participated in an interdenominational symposium on 'Women in the Clergy.' I asked him for his rationale. He answered that it is wrong for us to concede by default every debate to those who malign our position. He did not legitimize his opponents' credentials or point of view. He rationally explained 'our' point of view to an audience that would otherwise never have heard a Torah-true perspective.

"Perhaps, in 1996, we should try to find every possible way to reach Jews before they are even further away from any vestige of Jewish tradition. Can an Orthodox outreach group go into a non-Orthodox synagogue building to teach Hebrew, to explain *mitzvos*? Is there any variation depending on who asks the question and which city we are asking about? How broad is the *'issur'* (the prohibition against cooperation with the non-Orthodox movements)?"

The newer climate of opportunity for a more serious and authentic attitude towards Judaism is evident in the strangest places, usually in the press. It is only in the public eye that these changes in attitude can truly be identified. And as such, I feel that these public discussions regarding Judaism and the nature of American Jewry are truly indicative of the quiet revolution that I described earlier. It is a quest for self-identity, self-worth, for history and purpose and destiny. But the revolution will not gain greater momentum if it is ignored, or worse, denigrated, by the traditional Jewish camp that alone has the spiritual treasure to rebuild American Jewry.

Orthodoxy has long refused to accommodate Reform's changing definitions of Judaism or the Conservative movement's frantic attempts to maintain its spiritual balance on the slippery slope of nonhalachic Jewish faith. But that is no longer the issue. The issue is how Orthodoxy will respond to the opportunities now present to speak to the Jews who find themselves affiliated with these non-Orthodox movements. If we never speak to the "Federation Jews," if we never converse with, or more importantly, learn and study with non-Orthodox leaders and clergy, if we just write off two-thirds of American Jewry as being unworthy of our consideration and efforts, are we not the most guilty of all American Jews in abetting the spiritual destruction of our brothers and sisters? We and we alone possess the wherewithal to help and save them. But it will take a broader society than has been shown by official American Orthodoxy until now.

I am reminded of the comment made by one of my mentors in the yeshivah in Chicago 50 years ago. He said that in Lithuania there was a tradition that Rabbi Yisrael Lipkin of Salant, the founder of the great Mussar Movement of Jewish ethical and halachic renewal, commented: "Rabbi Moshe Sofer Schreiber (the Chasam Sofer) fought Reform by invoking a *cherem* (ban, anathema) against it and its adherents. My policy would have been to install a *beis midrash* (Talmudic study hall) in every Reform temple to teach Torah." Though I am not worthy to comment upon the policies of either Rabbi Moshe Sofer

Schreiber or Rabbi Yisrael Lipkin of Salant, or even upon the veracity of this tradition of Lithuanian Jewry, I think that the program allegedly proposed by Rabbi Yisrael Lipkin of Salant could prove successful in American Jewish life today. All of the successes of the *kiruv* organizations and the community *kollelim* in this country testify to the wisdom of such a program and to its infinite possibilities for strengthening Jewish identity and commitment in America. I am convinced that an outreach-oriented, nonjudgmental *kollel* placed on every college campus would do more to counteract intermarriage and Jewish alienation than all of the surveys, programs, and social events now being employed by the mainstream Jewish organizations. But such *kollelim* require people to staff them, and only Orthodoxy possesses the necessary reservoir of people.

The quiet revolution taking place now in American Jewry is in accord with the traditional, Biblical view of how Jewish life and destiny will unfold. The *pintele Yid,* the Jewish nucleus of soul that lies buried deep within every Jew, is very resistant to complete extinguishment. It revives itself in Jewish families that have been completely secular for generations. It gnaws at Jews wherever and however they live. It forces Jews to feel their uniqueness and perhaps even helps give rise to our all-too-common community neuroses. It fuels our aggressive drive to attempt continually to improve our society and our world. It gives us no rest and keeps us searching for our true selves and our roles in life. The quiet revolution is now in progress. Where it will lead depends in great measure upon our recognition of it and our positive response to its vast possibilities. It would be tragic and inexcusable if we missed this new, G–d-given opportunity to build American Jewry on the foundations of Torah and tradition.

Seeing Is Believing

Did you ever arrange to meet someone at a location which is one of the busiest intersections in town, always teeming with thousands of people? I am certain that you have done so. And isn't it remarkable how you are always able to recognize your companion, even from afar, even in the midst of that sea of strange humanity? This uncanny ability to discern one among many, familiar among foreign, the expected among the random, is attributable to one main fact — you were *looking* for that person. The ability to concentrate our minds and senses to find who and what we are searching for is a beneficial phenomenon of human life. A less beneficial phenomenon is the mirror trait of being able to ignore what we are *not* looking for, even when it stares us in the face. There is a sign that I saw in an executive office that summed up this matter so exquisitely. It said simply: "Don't confuse me with the facts — my mind is already made up."

Joseph and his brothers have been separated by distance for over two decades. They meet in Joseph's palace in Egypt, where he accuses them of being seditious spies. They indignantly and righteously deny this false accusation. Thus begins the drama of the reconciliation of Joseph and his family. In setting the scene for the unfolding series of events, the Torah states: "And Joseph recognized his brothers, but they did not recognize him." In this short descriptive sentence lies the entire explanation for the behavior of all of the parties concerned in this apparently bizarre and shocking story. Joseph, believing in the Divinely inspired dreams that he has nurtured within him his entire life, is *looking* for his brothers. He is waiting for them to appear before him and bow down to him, thereby fulfilling his vision of leadership amongst the tribes of Israel. He constantly scans the multitudes of customers who have come to Egypt to purchase grain. Amidst the tens of thousands of faces, he recognizes his brothers, even though they, like he, have aged over the years. He was *looking* for them, and therefore he found them.

The brothers were convinced that since Joseph's dreams were unacceptable to them, they could not be realized. They were unwilling to accommodate themselves, their life-styles, and personal goals to his dangerous dreams. They convinced themselves in advance, while Joseph was but 17, that the dreams and the dreamer had to be eliminated and that he must not be allowed the opportunity to prove himself worthy of those lofty dreams. Therefore, they could not see the viceroy of Egypt standing before them as Joseph. They ignored the truth staring them in the face because they were *not* looking for Joseph as a leader. Their minds were made up, and so the facts were ignored until the final climax of the story, when the truth could no longer be denied.

Much of human life is spent in this denial of reality. If we are *not* looking for self-improvement, spiritual growth, and a more wholesome existence, we will ignore and even denigrate the opportunities that stare us in the face. Jews who are still committed to outmoded social, economic, and political theories of the modern period, disproven by events and hollow in spiritual content, will never see their Joseph. Influenced by their childish view of Judaism (acquired at 12 or 13 and never since seriously studied or reexamined), they never allow themselves to renew the search for their heritage and their true inner selves. The redemption of Joseph's brothers occurs when they finally recognize him standing in front of them. The redemption of Jews lies in recognizing Judaism as a central, identifying foundation in their lives. Let us truly *look* for Torah in our daily existence.

Bad News

No one wants to hear bad news. Predictions of gloom and doom never receive an appreciative audience. We always want to believe the best and to feel somehow that the worst will not occur. This is equally true of nations and of individuals. Neville Chamberlain, at Munich in 1936, believed that "Herr Hitler was a man of his word"; Stalin refused to believe that Hitler would dare attack the Soviet Union even when presented by clear intelligence that the attack was imminent; Golda Meir and Moshe Dayan refused to believe the report of their intelligence experts that Assad and Sadat were about to unleash the Yom Kippur War on Israel; George Bush wistfully hoped that Saddam Hussein would disappear after the Gulf War; and a large part of the population of Israel and its government are hoping against hope that Arafat and the Palestinians are really ready for peace and cooperation with the Jewish state. Unfortunately, history is strewn with the wreckage of people and nations who refused to believe that their worst scenario could ever materialize. Distressing predictions are never to be totally ignored. They have a bad habit of being fulfilled.

The Torah completes the book of *Vayikra* by describing in deadly detail the possibility of the destruction of the Jewish national entity and the scattering of the Jewish people in a prolonged exile. Even though this *tochachah* — dire reproof and warning — is clearly and forcefully enunciated in the Torah, the Biblical commentators teach us that Israel did not take the warning too seriously. The Jewish people felt that G–d had too great a stake in the Land of Israel, the Holy Temple in Jerusalem, and the well-being of the nation to actually fulfill these threats. The Jews saw their situation as analogous to that of a debtor who has so much money on loan that the bank cannot force him into default and bankruptcy, lest the bank itself fail. But the Jews miscalculated. They did not take the bitter warnings and doleful predictions seriously. They hoped for the best while behaving their worst. And thus, when the *tochachah* was realized, they were doubly crushed by it. Not only were they punished severely for their iniquities, but they also suffered the embarrassment of having done nothing positive to save themselves when there was still time.

I am not a prophet nor the son of a prophet. As such, I do not know what the morrow brings for us; like everyone else, I hope for the best and attempt to be an optimist. But I think that a sense of realism amongst us is necessary for the Jewish world to survive. We are living witnesses in this century to the fact that the *tochachah* can occur. We also know by now that the Jewish people can be enormously "downsized" by the behavior of Jews themselves and their alienation from Torah. There are a lot of dire predictions about the viability of the Jewish people and the Jewish state in the next century. These assessments should be taken seriously and acted upon in order to assure that they do not happen. Better sure than sorry. This is not a popular policy, and no one wants to hear about problems when they would rather hear soothing words and rosy assurances. But it would be foolhardy and suicidal to ignore our history and the reality of *tochachah* which the Torah portrays for us. Forewarned is forearmed. The confidence that Torah life inspires within us gives us the strength to look at our situation realistically and thus triumph in our personal and national lives.

Laws and Legality

A great deal of human cruelty and perversity is based on the rule of law. In our century we have been witness to the justification for some of the worst human behavior in history by the use of excuses such as "I was just following orders" or "I was just enforcing the law." That was Eichmann's defense of his efficiency in organizing the slaughter of millions, of the Communist *apparatchiks* who destroyed an entire society, of sadistic police the world over who use their power to brutalize others. We cannot exist without the rule of law. However, the traditional rule of law of civilized societies can be perverted. George Orwell named the murderous secret police in his fictional (but unerringly true to life) totalitarian society "The Department of Love." Law alone is not the safeguard of society and human values. A sense of morality and an inner compass that points to right and wrong are the true guarantees of the justness of the rule of law in human affairs.

The Torah contains the admonition "You shall not do evil (perversity) in the exercise of justice (legislation, courts, police, government, etc.)." The Torah here repeats one of its constant themes: Justice is served only by acting justly. There are no just ends that support the use of unjust means. The law is never to be used for evil purposes. G–d's demand for moral behavior takes precedence over all rules and laws. Ramban, in his great commentary on the Bible, states: "One should beware not to be a *naval b'reshus haTorah* (a base person who is technically observing the law of the Torah)." He further states: "This is the pattern of our Torah — after stating the laws of judges, courts, and monetary and business matters, and cautioning us not to steal or to be otherwise [legally or technically] dishonest, it then demands of us that we live up to the great general rule 'And you shall do what is just and good in the eyes of the L–rd your G–d.' One should introduce into his behavior the moral rightness and fairness and do *more than the law demands* in order to accommodate his fellow human beings." Only when such an attitude becomes second nature to us can we hope to fulfill this Biblical injunction of not doing evil in the (seeming) exercise of justice. One cannot look at the law as being detached from life's circumstances, as being somehow above the fray; that is how evil is perpetrated through the law. One must always see the consequences of the law's application, and if those consequences are unjust, evil, or immoral, the Torah rejects that path.

But how are we to know in advance the consequences of following the law? Moreover, how are we to know what is right and what is wrong, what is good and what is bad, in a society that changes its standards so capriciously? An answer to that question was offered in the 19th century by Kant and others, who claimed that man and man alone is capable of deciding these issues. After the disasters of the 20th century, we are no longer so sure of man's ability to chart an effective moral course for the individual and society. Wilhelm, Nicholas, Hitler, Lenin, Stalin, Pol Pot, Mao, Sadaam Hussein, to name a few of the "legalists" of the 20th century, have disabused us of the notion of human morality existing independently. The Torah's morality is based on the will of G–d. It subscribes to G–d's definitions of right, wrong, good, and evil. "You shall do what is right and good in the eyes of the L–rd your G–d" is the Jewish method of not perverting legality into evil. It alone allows us to be certain that what we believe to be good and right now will also be seen as good and right by our descendants generations later.

Free Speech

Free speech is an integral part of a free society. Yet, like all freedoms, it requires responsibility and self-discipline in its exercise. Justice Oliver Wendell Holmes, in his famous Supreme Court opinion, declared that freedom of speech does not allow one to shout "fire" in a crowded theater where no fire exists. Thus, even this most free of all our freedoms, the right to say what we wish, must be subject to some limitations in order for society to function.

Nevertheless, we are witness daily to outrageous slanders, both personal and communal, that fill our media. Gossip columnists are folk heroes even if they are consistently wrong and vicious in their reports. We are so enamored of the affairs of others that the concept of the right to personal privacy, especially for people in the public eye, has been shredded. Personal attacks, slanderous statements, and dubious opinions about others are all now acceptable in our society. The cost of such behavior is, in my opinion, inestimable, and it is the source of much of what is wrong in Jewish life in America and Israel today.

The Torah deals with wretched types of dermatological diseases (whatever they were, they did not include leprosy) that require spiritual cleansing in order for the afflicted person to be healed and to become ritually pure once more. Our Rabbis stated that these diseases were caused by a spiritual failing — the sin of *lashon hara*, "evil speech." The Torah bids us not to speak about other human beings. The Talmud indicates that there are instances when even apparently complimentary speech about others is not permitted. We all know how derogatory faint praise and snide compliments can be. The Talmud realized that this problem of uninhibited freedom of speech was so all-encompassing that it stated that all human beings are somehow covered by the "dust of *lashon hara.*" In the last century, the sainted Rabbi Yisrael Meir Kagan wrote a number of great books detailing the laws of speech and how to avoid the trap of speaking *lashon hara.* A great effort was made, and is still being made, in the traditional Jewish world to speak in an acceptable and refined holy fashion. There is no room for slander in life. The exposé, whether oral or in print, usually leaves the speaker more exposed than the victim. Our rabbis taught us that *lashon hara* "kills" three victims — the speaker, the listener, and the subject of the conversation. Uninhibited speech leads to bad consequences.

The characteristic that distinguishes humans from animals is the power of speech, which, more than any other trait, represents our intellectual capacity to communicate. Judaism always has taught that this characteristic is a holy gift from the Creator. Just like the gifts of life, health, talents, and family, this gift of speech is not to be abused. It is to be used sparingly and carefully, for good purposes and not for evil. Gossip, muckraking, slander, and cynical language all fly in the face of the purpose of this holy gift of speech. Even when one is speaking the truth, one is cautioned to avoid the pitfalls of *lashon hara,* for unlike the case of a libel action, truth alone is not a sufficient cause for speaking about others. As such, the rabbinic encouragement of healthy silence is well understood and appreciated. In a world where, sadly, this precept is in vogue, and in fact, the entire concept of *lashon hara* may inspire only incredulity, a determined effort on our part to restore the sanctity of speech is certainly in order.

Ideals and Details

It was a wise man who said that "the devil is in the details." As a lawyer, I became painfully aware that general agreements and apparent meetings of the mind often came undone in the formulation of the details. All of the great general hopes and desires of life — love, family, career, kindness, purpose — are subject to the modification of details. And if the details don't work out, then the grandest and noblest ideas, goals, and theories are meaningless.

After the great ideas and declamations of the Ten Commandments — ideas to which all of Israel pledged loyalty and obedience — the Torah fleshed out those great principles with the details of how they were to be applied in everyday behavior. It is one thing to subscribe to the concept of honesty and kindness, but how does that concept translate into behavior in adversarial business relationships? Everyone wants to be a kind and efficient boss, but how is that possible in a world of labor unions, recalcitrant employees, and intense financial pressures? I want to be a good neighbor, but what if my neighbor is raucous or disturbing to me and my property? Do fences really make for good neighbors? And what does the G–d of Israel really mean by saying that "you shall not steal"? What are the rules regarding competition, advertising, and proper profit-pricing? How about interest and usury, banking fees, and net discounts for early payments on purchases? And what is our *true and real* obligation towards the poor, the widow, the orphans, the homeless, and the sick? We all wish to be good people and to serve our Creator, but how can we actualize this desire in our everyday lives? Ah, those pesky details!

The Talmud teaches us that if one wishes to be reckoned a *chasid,* a truly pious person, he must fulfill the details, the minutiae of the laws of the Talmudic order of *nezikin. Nezikin* concerns itself with all of the laws that appear in *Mishpatim,* which deal with relationships between people as enunciated in the Ten Commandments given at Sinai. There is no hope for true piety and service of G–d without working out every aspect of the details. For the holiness of Jewish life lies solely in those details.

We have been witness too often to great and lofty ideals that were transfigured into horror and tyranny because no one was able to work out those details. It is therefore no act of caprice that Jewish children throughout the ages were initiated into the mysteries and glory of Talmudic study by beginning with *Nezikin.* There are simpler places for novices to begin their study of Talmud. But Jews knew that the purpose of Talmudic study was not merely the acquisition of knowledge and intellect, but rather the development of holiness, goodness, and piety. As such, our children had to get right down to the details immediately, to deal with practical and not merely theoretical goodness, to try and become a *chasid* by dealing with G–dly details and not just pious generalities. *Mishpatim* is the rock of goodness upon which all Jewish ideas of fairness and kindness among people are based. This *parshah* is worthy of our continued attention, study, and fulfillment.

I Need, I Want, I Deserve ...

Of all the Ten Commandments — the *aseres hadibros* — that are recorded in the Torah, I think the most difficult one to observe, or even comprehend, is the final one, *lo sachmod,* not to covet or desire what belongs to others. How is one to control his innate nature, which always desires what others have? How can the Torah ask of humans to achieve the seemingly impossible? And, perhaps most fundamental of all, what is so *wrong* about coveting, longing for better things and more of them, even if they are possessed by others? After all, to the victor belongs the spoils, and those who are successful should have the right to claim the prize even if it is at the expense of the less successful. This has certainly been the prevailing view in society for centuries, and human talent has unfortunately always been expended to justify the acquisition of territory, wealth, and possessions of others. So how do we understand the nature of this prohibition against wanting what belongs to others?

Rabbi Avraham ibn Ezra, in his commentary on the Bible, states that G–d's commandment not to covet is to create within us the understanding that it is beyond our ken to expect to acquire anything that is not ours. He says that just as the peasant does not aspire in reality to marry the princess and therefore does not really covet her — for one covets only what he can reasonably expect to acquire — so too should we not covet whatever does not belong to us, for the commandment of G–d designates that object as the unattainable "princess." However psychologically palatable ibn Ezra's idea was in his time, it does not resonate easily in our time, conditioned as we are to believe that everyone is entitled to compete for the "princess" and that even the commonest of peasants can win her hand. Thus, our generation must perceive this difficult commandment in a different light in order to relate to G–d's word positively and to see it as relevant.

Perhaps the key to this commandment lies in our understanding of coveting. The Torah's view may be that that coveting involves obsessive, compulsive, single-minded desire. "I can't live without it" is the type of coveting that is most destructive in society. The truth in life is that one can "live without" most objects, and even without most people, that we so strongly desire. This is the strong dash of cold reality that allows us to control our acquisitive instincts. Thus, coveting is forced back into the recesses of our psyches and does not dominate us. Unchecked coveting always leads to antisocial behavior in individuals, and to terrible wars when it occurs in nations and groups.

The Talmud states that when one steals, he violates not only the prohibition against stealing but the prohibition against coveting as well. Thus, stealing becomes coveting realized, as adultery is coveting realized, as murder also is ultimately coveting realized. Not coveting, therefore, means seeing life in perspective, being moderate and not compulsive, tranquil and not aggressive, satisfied and not constantly frustrated. It is the key to mental health and normal behavior in societies. Not coveting is certainly relevant and important to all of us and to our world.

Creation and Creativity

The seasons of the year regularly roll round, and we begin every year with the Torah reading of *Bereishis* — the beginning not only of the yearly cycle of Torah readings, but the beginning of *everything!* As the science of astrophysics has gained momentum in our generation, and as we have a better understanding of the universe — its unbelievable immensity, regularity, and force — the words of the Torah describing the beginning of everything take on even more significance and vitality. The universe is larger, more complex, yet more ordered and organized than ever imagined by previous generations. And it is probably safe to say that a century from now, astrophysicists will view our current knowledge of the universe as primitive and faulty. Yet one thing is certain, and that is that the universe developed in such a quick fashion — only seconds — that to believe it was a random product of accident is really stretching all logic. However, there are many famous scientists who do believe in this randomness, and this is merely another example of G–d's having granting man free will and choice; and one can therefore believe or dis-believe whatever he wishes, irrespective of logic.

Judaism is built upon the belief in a Creator of the universe and of life itself. Perhaps the greatest contribution of Judaism to general civilization is this concept of a Creator Who is the source of all that we can observe and all that remains unob-served in our universe. Modern astrophysicists estimate that we have observed barely *three* percent of the universe in our ex-amination of space. Is that not what G–d told Moses when He said, "Man, who is alive, will never be able to see me?" G–d, as Creator, is not accessible or comprehensible to man, no matter how advanced our technology or how incisive our scientific the-ories become. But G–d as our Father, our personal Guide, Who is interested in us and our actions, Who has revealed Himself to us over many millennia of Jewish life, is present and always ac-cessible. Moses told Israel, "Who is like the L–rd our G–d, Who is always close to us whenever we call unto him?" It is one of the tragedies of modern life that because G–d the Creator is be-yond our ability to understand and to know, we also somehow have given up on G–d our Father, Who is our personal guide and companion in life and death. It is as though one has two keys to enter a great mansion, and when he is unable to open the gate with one of the keys, he simply walks away without even attempting to open the gate with the other key — the one that does work.

The Torah tells us very little about G–d the Creator. The story of creation as described in *Bereishis* is purposely vague and incom-plete. G–d does not share His secrets with us easily. In fact, G–d does not play the main "role" in the Torah — man does. The Torah describes itself as being "the book of man." Man is the focus of the story of civilization, perhaps even of the entire universe. The Torah demands of man a moral life, a purposeful life, an eternal life. The story of *Bereishis* is therefore the story of Adam and Eve, of Cain and Abel, of the difficulties of civilization, and of the problem of remaining godly and vital in a world that is far from being the Garden of Eden. The mystery of human behavior is no less a puzzle than that of the creation of the universe. We may not solve the riddle of the universe, but it is within our power to improve human behavior — our own behavior.

Justice and Compassion

One of the basic rules of Jewish jurisprudence is *adam muad l'olam* — every individual is fully liable and responsible for his behavior. Though there is extensive halachic literature regarding liability or the lack thereof for *grama,* less-than-direct causation of damage to others, there is no provision for what we popularly call an "accident." The rule of the Talmud is that one is liable for damages caused directly to others whether they be intentional or unintentional, whether consciously caused or unconsciously perpetrated (such as in one's sleep). This unbending view of personal liability for one's actions is not limited to issues of torts and damages, but lies at the heart of the Jewish view of life. It speaks against the ever present, popular rationalization of evil and of destructive attitudes and behavior in society. It limits our inclination to blame others, society, circumstances, for our own personal shortcomings and guilt. It is a painful doctrine, both legally and psychologically.

It is interesting that Judaism constantly preaches mercy and forgiveness towards wrongdoers and wayward people. This is an extension of its doctrine of *imitatio Dei*, the mandate to imitate the ways of the Creator. If that be the case, how is the previously described doctrine of no-excuse liability reconcilable with this precept of forgiveness and compassion toward others? Those who demand "law and order" are always perceived as somewhat lacking in compassion. If no "accidents" are allowed in life, how can society survive? How can we cope with such a rigid and fearsome code of justice?

The great scholars of Israel have discussed this problem over the centuries, and I take the liberty and risk of oversimplifying their answer. We all know that in current legal practice, in both civil and criminal matters, there are two separate phases of a trial. One deals with the guilt or innocence, liability or lack thereof, of the accused. The other phase deals with the punishment of the accused, if and when that person is found guilty of the charges. During the first phase, all excuses or rationalizations for the behavior of the defendant are irrelevant and inadmissible. The question is reduced to its simplest and starkest form: Did the defendant commit the act he is charged with? If he did, then the rule of *adam muad l'olam*, one is always responsible for his behavior, prevails. There are no "accidents" in human behavior. One either did or did not commit the act. It is that simple and that brutal.

But even if one is liable for the act, the second phase of the trial must now take place. In that part of the proceedings, both in earthly and in courts, the motivations, circumstances, excuses, and "accidents" that are so much a part of human existence are taken into account and factored into the punishment meted out to the guilty party. Here the G–d of compassion and mercy is present, and all mitigating circumstances are accounted for. The rights of society and of the defendant are reconciled, and the holy verdict of G–d's perfect judgment emerges. Only G–d can perform perfect justice, but by understanding this basic law of Jewish jurisprudence, we may also glimpse His righteous ways.

X
MUSINGS —
SOME AMUSING

Something's Fishy

An Israeli fisherman, Yaakov Ezri, dipped his trawling net into Lake Kinneret (The Sea of Galilee) in 1994 and, together with the usual catch of carp, pulled out three interlopers, "savage-looking and six inches long... [with] sharp teeth and...the eyes of carnivores. By accident or some sinister plot, man-eating piranhas (whose natural abode is in tropical Brazil) had come to Israel." This was the story published then in *The Washington Post*, which also made note of the fact that Israel Radio treated Ezri's find as serious news. This in turn provoked a feeding frenzy in Israel's tabloid press, always looking for their obligatory Orthodox Jew-bites–dog story, but willing to settle for piranhas when necessary. "*Maariv* ran a two page spread headlined 'Piranha Panic,'" reported the *Post*. "'The smell of blood excites them,' said Menachem Goren, a professor at Tel Aviv University, apparently speaking of the fish and not the press," the *Post* dryly noted. *Maariv* turned Goren's quotation into an inch-tall headline. A TV talk-show host invited an expired piranha to appear on his program, dutifully accompanied by a bureaucrat from the

Department of Fisheries of the State of Israel. Even in death, the fish, and especially its teeth, received rave reviews. The bureaucrat's performance was only fair in comparison, and he was largely ignored by the Israeli TV critics. Fame is fleeting and fickle!

The *Post* reported: "Questions abounded. Were these fishy fugitives from an aquarium? Pawns of a foreign power? Would Israel demand a crackdown by Yassir Arafat?" The director of Israel's Agricultural Ministry said that whoever was guilty of introducing killer piranhas into Lake Kinneret had committed "a grave infraction of the law." The mayor of Tiberias, Yossi Peretz, called for public aplomb. "I hope it becomes clear that we're not talking about a dangerous fish at all and that everyone will calm down" was his wistful statement. Zvi Ortenberg, a Galilean fisherman, claimed to have been bitten by a piranha while fishing on Lake Kinneret. *Maariv* promptly headlined: "Killer Fish Bites Kinneret Fisherman." Kashrus-certifying organizations instructed their supervisors in Israeli fish-processing plants to be on the lookout for the killer fish (a non-kosher species?) which may have somehow infiltrated the processing plants, its jaws embedded in a carp destined for gefilte fish. The tension mounted as the government solemnly announced, "Clearly this can hurt tourism, in which we've invested so much over the years."

But alas, as we all know, things in Israel are never really quite as they appear. Daniel Golani, the expert Israeli ichthyologist, and curator of the fish collection of Jerusalem's Hebrew University, was put on the case. After examining the dead specimens of the Kinneret piranha, he pronounced the creature from Brazil to be an impostor. "The teeth were all wrong. Piranha teeth look like little blades, the better to tear meat. The teeth on this fish were sharp and strong, but they were made to cut through only plants and nuts." Golani clearly adjudicated the matter: "This is no piranha. It is a common pieu, a distant cousin of the piranha." The Israeli press trumpeted his reassuring findings. The great piranha scare ended. The country could now return to worrying about its usual problems of Arab terrorism, Jewish divisiveness, and government by committee. A sigh of relief was heard throughout the Holy Land.

Where Are My Reading Glasses?

Ever since that dreaded day years ago when the ophthalmologist confirmed what my eyes had been telling me for months — namely, that I needed glasses, at least for reading — one of the major questions of life reverberating in my home has been "Where are my reading glasses?" People who wear glasses all the time probably always know where their glasses are — on their noses. But some people such as me, who in their vanity wear glasses "only" for reading, writing, and close work, can never find them. After about a year of domestic frustration and tension about where my glasses were and whose job it was to keep track of those elusive spectacles, I devised a foolproof scheme to solve the problem. I bought extra pairs of glasses. I have a pair of glasses in my weekday *tallis* bag, in my Sabbath *tallis* bag, in my cubby at the synagogue, in my office at the yeshivah, on my bedroom reading table, in my dresser drawer, and naturally in my suit pocket.

So how come I was forced to conduct a wedding ceremony recently in front of hundreds of unusually attentive onlookers without my glasses to aid me in preparing the necessary documents and reading the ceremonial blessings properly? There is nothing as demeaning to rabbinic dignity as having to plaintively shout in public, "Where are my reading glasses?"

Last Chanukah my wife and I traveled to South Bend, Indiana, to visit our children and grandchildren. Upon arriving at La Guardia Airport, brimming with pride that I had remembered to bring the airplane tickets with me, I discovered in horror that I had forgotten my reading glasses somewhere. To have to exist for three days without being able to read, write, or study, especially in the presence of my grandchildren, who think highly of me, is cruel and unusual punishment. But it was certainly too late to go home to fetch my glasses, and anyway, I didn't remember where they were in the house, or I wouldn't have forgotten them in the first place. So I reconciled myself to the fate of having to share my wife's reading glasses with her (she never forgets where her glasses are), which is certainly an imperfect solution — both optical and marital — to the problem. But, all rumors to the contrary notwithstanding, the good L–rd is always on the side of rabbis. I discovered a gift shop in the airport terminal building which, for some inexplicable reason, stocked generic reading glasses and was willing to sell them to the public for exorbitant prices. Gratefully paying $20 for two 50-cent lenses, I added another pair of reading glasses to my ever increasing collection.

In the belief that I am not alone in this problem, I have taken the liberty of sharing these experiences with you. Any advice or suggestions that you may have for me as to how to deal with this vexing life problem will be most appreciated. I only hope that I am able to find my reading glasses in time to be able to read your letters, which I am certain will be full of good advice and wise suggestions.

On Neckties

The last refuge of accepted masculine vanity is the necktie. This piece of clothing, which serves no useful or practical purpose whatsoever, has come to define the personality and self-perception of the wearer. Thus, there is a "power" tie (usually red or yellow), a "dress" tie (usually black or white), and myriad ties for different occasions and moods. Even rabbis, whose traditional dress code of dark suits and white shirts proscribes any real fashion statements, have retained some freedom of choice regarding neckties. The truth is that most men, including rabbis, are really hooked on ties.

What inspires these ruminations on such a weighty topic was my rash grandfatherly promise to my grandsons to purchase neckties for them as a memento of my trip to Hong Kong. Along with ties for my father and son, I found myself in the position of having to purchase close to 20 ties on a limited budget, a not-insignificant challenge. I discovered a tie stand on the sidewalk of one of Hong Kong's famous "tourist trap" shopping streets. I am not a good bargainer, and in fact I dislike haggling when purchasing anything. But here I was, faced by the challenge of my shopping life. I coolly appraised more than 600 ties hanging on the racks surrounding the stand and began to pick out the ones that I thought would be most appropriate for my scholarly, but somehow very fashion-conscious, family. After choosing a different tie for each relative (you never give brothers or cousins the same tie), I asked the dreaded question: "How much?"

The Chinese merchant sized me up immediately and said, "Five ties for 100 Hong Kong dollars." I pointed out the large sign hanging in front of his stand, which read: "*Six* (italics mine) ties for $100." He responded that this ridiculously low price applied only to the regular ties that he had for sale, but that I had chosen the most elegant ties in his inventory and that he was really losing money selling me those beauties even at the higher price. Flattered at his recognition of my superb taste in ties, I was tempted to give in then and there; but from the facial expression of the seller, I realized that he expected me to make a dramatic counteroffer to his proposition. Not wishing to be impolite, I weakly offered him five and a half ties for 100 Hong Kong dollars. The look of disgust on his face shamed me, but he saved me any further embarrassment by informing me that since I was buying in such volume, he would sell me 21 ties for 300 Hong Kong dollars. I immediately picked out another two ties, paid the money, and made my escape with my ties, chuckling to myself at my coup; I had purchased seven ties for 100 Hong Kong dollars. Of course, I now had two more ties than I had intended to buy, but, my friends, a rabbi can never own too many ties.

However, as I left the shopping street, my peripheral vision caught sight of a sign hanging on another necktie stand that I had overlooked. The sign said: "Quality neckties, *nine* (italics mine) for 100 Hong Kong dollars." I pretended to ignore the sign and hustled my wife and my 21 ties out of that street of heartbreak as fast as I could. But in my heart I had the feeling common to everyone who gets a "bargain" — I had been had.

Discussing ties reminds me of a traumatic event of my early yeshivah days in Chicago. Almost all of the young men in my class were poor by today's standards of affluence. We each owned one necktie apiece, and certainly not a designer one at that. When we began searching for our future spouses, we all had a meeting and decided that we would pool our meager assets and purchase one really good, colorful silk tie for common use. We agreed to hold a lottery to decide who would get to wear "the tie" when, and to schedule our social life accordingly. We were certain that "the tie" would certainly make each one of us more attractive, if not downright irresistible, to the young lady in question. After three or four of us had worn "the tie" with varying success, an incident occurred that ended the experiment. One of my friends came back from a meeting with a girl, in whom he was particularly interested, looking crestfallen and somewhat depressed. I asked him what had gone wrong, and he told me mournfully that the girl had said, "I went out once before with that tie!" So much for magic ties.

Ties are also a vehicle for male bonding. Teaching one's son how to tie a necktie properly is an emotional and traditional moment and represents the passing on of a necessary skill to the next generation. Most sons, in their heart of hearts, do not really approve of their fathers' taste in ties, and when they become old enough to choose their own ties, they will invariably rebel against the adult styles previously chosen for them.

And the wonderful thing about ties is that the styles all become obsolete in a very short period of time. Ties change from narrow to wide and back again with alarming speed and regularity. Therefore, many men never throw out old ties, hoping that they will return to current fashion once again. But the true tie aficionado is always on the lookout for a new tie that will make the correct statement about his true personality. I have received many more compliments from my congregants about my ties than about my sermons. There is a message in that somewhere, but I have never pursued it too deeply. I appreciate the winning value of a good tie, and I look forward to many more intriguing tie-purchasing situations in the future. I am also mightily grateful to the L–rd for having allowed me to purchase ties for four generations of males in my family — all at the same time.

My Best Friend

When we are small children, we treasure the concept of having a "best friend." A child that does not have a best friend feels socially deprived. As we grow older, we find substitutes for a best friend in our lives. But all of these substitutes, even a spouse, children, business partners, doctors and therapists, are never best friend. I am writing this article now because my own best friend died last month, and now I no longer have one. This leads me to consider the nature of friends, why they are so important to us, and the true definition and meaning of friendship. I find that the search for this definition is a difficult and wrenching one, for it involves a deep self-analysis on my part. To define friendship in my own personal terms means also to define who I am. To tell you the truth, I have not looked at myself that way in a very long time.

The Bible is replete with stories of friends and friendship. From these, one can infer the nature of true friendship and how it transcends ordinary human inhibitions, embarrassments, and weaknesses. Judah, the leader of the sons of Jacob, is despondent over the sale of Joseph. He withdraws from the company of his brothers and bonds with his friend, Hiram the Addulamite. Judah becomes ensnared in the consequences of his meeting with Tamar. It is certainly a difficult matter for him to recount the meeting with Tamar, whom he judged to be a woman of ill repute, and to admit that she held his seal and identification as collateral for payment of her fee. Nevertheless, he does recount this entire embarrassing incident to Hiram and asks him for help in resolving the matter, because Hiram was a friend.

A friend may be critical of one's behavior, but a true friend is never judgmental. Thus, a friend essentially allows one to develop and grow, to admit errors and weep over tragedies, to be honest and forthcoming, and to deal with the realities of life and its problems. A friend such as this eventually becomes a "best friend" — one who harbors no illusions and bears no grudges, has a long memory but is short on harping recollections, and fulfills his role without reward or conditions.

The Mishnah teaches us that the prime Biblical example of selfless unconditional and unlimited love is the friendship between Jonathan and David. It is a love that transcends one's personal interests and welfare. Jonathan is the heir to the throne of Israel, the logical and popular successor to his father, King Saul. Saul himself warns Jonathan that David is the rival who will end their family's royal dynasty before it is really able to solidify itself. In effect, Saul tells Jonathan to choose between David and himself. And Jonathan chooses David, even over his own interest and those of his family. This is more than selflessness — it is an altruism that almost transcends the imagination of us ordinary mortals.

I feel that the Rabbis, in using Jonathan and David as the paragon of friendship, were illustrating for us its unlimited nature. Such a friendship knows no boundaries of self, family, conditions, or circumstances. A true best friend is very elusive quarry. Therefore, when one does find such a person, the Rabbis encourage that selfless, almost self-denying relationship in spite of its risks. For it seems that having a best friend is not a luxury, but is more in the nature of a necessity. As such, the example of David and Jonathan is properly advanced as the ideal.

My best friend recently passed away in his Jerusalem home. I had seen him two weeks before his death. As is many times the case in such instances, we both sensed that this would more than likely be our last meeting in this world. Yet we did not discuss items of great import, satisfied rather simply to be in one another's company. I thought then that one of the great qualities of friendship is the ability to maintain a comfortable silence in conversation. The lack of embarrassment that often accompanies silence in other social situations is one of the hallmarks of true friendship. It is what we did not say to each other at our last meeting that mattered. We did not have to remind ourselves verbally of the events of our 48 years of friendship. We shared many memories, some of them sad and tragic, others exhilarating and even hilarious. Our families had become intertwined with each other. His death, needless to say, leaves a great sadness within me. I am blessed beyond belief with my family, my colleagues, my career, tasks, and projects, and I am enormously grateful for my blessings. But I no longer have a best friend.

The Value of a Home

My wife and I were in the midst of the wrenching task of selling the home that we had lived in happily for 21 years. Selling a home is always a difficult experience. In our married life we have sold three homes in Chicago, moved from two homes in Miami Beach, and sold our first home in Monsey. Our home in Monsey was beautiful, spacious, comfortable, warm, and cozy. It had suited us just fine, and we had grown attached to it in a personal way. Like every home, the house had memories and emotions tucked into each corner. Our children were courted and married from this home. We celebrated their *sheva berachos seudos* (nuptial gatherings and meals during the week after the wedding) in this house, as well as many a family Pesach *seder* and Sabbath meal. Many of our grandchildren had spent their first weeks of life in under the shelter of this roof, and, by G–d's grace and kindness to our family, four generations had studied, laughed, played, and eaten together. How can one not love such a home and all that it represents?

But when one is planning to move to Jerusalem, even the most sentimental attachment to a home is worth the sacrifice. Therefore, my wife and I placed our home for sale in the real estate market of our community. The value of our home, in terms of dollars, had declined precipitously over the past five years. Its appraised value was only 55% of what it had been in 1991! When the real estate broker glumly informed us of the price she thought the house would fetch, a feeling of disappointment touched me. I was not going to be on Easy Street financially, after all; after 40 years in the rabbinate, I basically would only have broken even.

But then I read an opinion piece in the March 17, 1997 issue of *Newsweek* magazine, written by Patricia O'Keefe-Condon. The op-ed piece was called "A Home's True Worth." Never was an article written more directly to me and for my benefit! The subtitle of the article read: "Our old family house was a great investment in happy memories, not in moneymaking." O'Keefe-Condon wrote: "My neighbor is young, probably half my age, and I suppose the generation gap also includes the idea that money invested should always grow. Today many people live above their incomes in expensive homes. Their latchkey kids have matching beepers, and the microwave works overtime as both parents struggle to support it all. What is a home to the younger generation?

"Is it really just a financial investment? A profitmaking business? Shouldn't a home be a place of memories — memories that will take us through life, directing, always teaching, supporting? Is home no longer a place of comfort?" She concluded her beautiful article with the following idea: "After we were grown and had all moved out, my mother sold our old house for a song. She and my father had bought it for a song. What an investment!"

Well, my wife and I had bought this house of ours 21 years ago for a song. And it appears pretty clear at this point that we will sell it for a song. But what a song! The Torah compares our lives, in fact, all of Jewish history and the Torah itself, to a song. A song has high notes and low notes. In modern life, it may also contain discordant notes and periods of atonality. A house is also witness to high notes and low notes, laughter and tears, dissent and dissonance, melody and harmony. In short, a house accompanies us through life and is witness to all of its vicissitudes. We have known great joy and good health, thank G–d, in our home. We have also heard tragic news, suffered searing disappointments, and shed many tears there. We love our home and all that it has meant to us. I see in it every day beloved people, family and friends who are no longer with us. Their pictures on the wall are moving with us to Jerusalem, but the comfort of having identified them with the place will have to be left behind. Our house sings a song to us, loud and clear, comforting, laden with meaning and hope. That emotion is not measurable in terms of monetary value. A home's true worth, if measured only in money, is cheapened more profoundly than it can be by any volatility in the real estate market.

But every time I come to Jerusalem, I have a profound sense of being home. Even when I visit streets and places in the Holy City that I know I have never been to before, I have the feeling of familiarity, comfort, and serenity that only an old, well-lived-in home can convey. I have been trying for the past 30 years to go home. The declining real estate value of a house should never be sufficient reason to give up on a lifelong dream. Our old home has served us well. We will sell it for a song in order to be able to hear and be strengthened by an even more emotional song. At the Pesach *seder* we all declare: "Next year in Jerusalem!" Just imagine the joy and fulfillment of being able to declare at this year's *seder*: "This coming year in Jerusalem!" It is a special blessing to be able to go home.

Is Your Synagogue a "Ten"?

recently came across the Friday issue of a well-known Jerusalem Hebrew newspaper. I noticed that a reporter by the name of Yakov Levy reviews Jerusalem synagogues in a feature column appropriately titled "Yakov's Ladder" (Sulam Yakov). The writer, who characterizes himself, if modestly, as a "*chevraman*" (an untranslatable Yiddish word used in modern Hebrew to denote someone who is completely with it and knows all the ins and outs of absolutely everything), visits a different synagogue in Jerusalem every Sabbath morning and rates its services for his public on a scale from one to ten. It so happened that the one review I saw concerned Levy's visit to Beit Knesset HaNasi, located in the Rechavia section of Jerusalem on Rechov Ussishkin. Since that is the synagogue that I attend and deliver lectures in when I am in my Jerusalem home, I was more than curious to read Levy's review.

The main criteria for success in Levy's review are 1) warmth and hospitality to strangers, 2) good, a melodious, diction-accurate *chazan* and *baal kriah* (leaders of the prayer services and the public Torah reading), 3) well-paced services without annoying time-breaks, and 4) overall appearance of the synagogue and the level of decorum and dignity (not formal stiffness) of the services. Not a bad list of meaningful synagogue criteria, if I say so myself. He rated Beit Knesset HaNasi as an eight and recommended it highly, especially to strangers and first-timers, because of the conscious efforts of the officers and leaders to make newcomers feel welcome.

I was told by a friend of mine that he once was mistaken for a newspaper restaurant critic when he arrived at an upscale kosher restaurant in Manhattan. He said that he had never received such fine service and courteous attention as he did at that restaurant. He returned the next week, but this time his cover was blown, for the restaurant owner had now correctly identified him as a mere mortal and not a restaurant critic. He was treated "normally" and did not receive nearly the level of attention and care shown him previously. Too bad for the restaurant, because a good customer is often more valuable in the long run than a good newspaper review.

I think that we should place a notice in all synagogues that there may be a reviewer in attendance to rate the services. Undoubtedly, the attention and welcome to strangers, the warmth of the atmosphere, and the decorum of the prayer services would all be enhanced. If we could see a rating of ourselves and the performance of our houses of worship, I think it would promote improvement, though it could certainly be a sobering experience. Yakov Levy, keep it up; you have a good idea going there. We should all keep on climbing Yakov's ladder.

A Child's War Far from the Battlefield

Any American who is 60 years or older can remember where he or she was and what was happening on that fateful day of December 7, 1941, when the radio first notified the United States that it was at war. The course of all our lives was changed by that tragic moment in history. I was a child returning home from a Sunday-afternoon excursion with my mother when the news broke upon us as we entered our apartment on the West Side of

Chicago. I did not sleep well that night, imagining Japanese bombers over Chicago.

I had been conditioned by my parents' conversations over the years to think that war with Germany was inevitable, for Hitler meant to destroy our family because we were Jewish, even though he didn't really know us. I couldn't imagine that he would really want to do that because my mother and father, grandfather, aunts and uncles and cousins were all such wonderful people. But even if I couldn't understand it, I believed my parents' pronouncements that Hitler and Germany were our sworn enemies and that we would have to fight them. But who were the Japanese? Why were they fighting us? And how were we going to be able to beat both Germany and Japan at the same time, since I could see on my little world globe in my bedroom that they were on opposite sides of the world?

But the worst part of the war for me was seeing the anguish on the faces of my family as the story of the destruction of European Jewry became known. In 1943 we already knew that my father's brother, a respected rabbi in a small but prestigious town in Lithuania, and his entire family had been killed. After the war, we were told by eyewitnesses that my uncle, aunt, and cousins had in fact been killed not by the Germans but by Russian Communist commissars who accompanied the Red Army into Lithuania in 1940-41, eliminating many of the religious leaders and clergy who were certainly an "undesirable element opposing progress and the true freedom and education of the masses." Our home was never the same after that tragic news reached us. There was a subdued but omnipresent sadness that permeated my world. Every day we followed the radio and newspaper reports of the war. I am still addicted to the news because of that pattern established in childhood.

My grandfather had neighbors who had a son serving with the U.S. Marines in the Pacific. That young man was killed in the American assault on Saipan, one of the stepping-stone islands on the way to Iwo Jima, the Philippines, Okinawa, and eventually Japan. I was in my grandfather's home when the dreaded telegram from the Navy Department arrived at the neighbor's apartment just below us. The ashen look of desolation on my grandfather's face as he descended to their apartment to strengthen them in their ordeal remains with me to this day. As a child, hearing the wailing and screaming from the neighbor's apartment on that sad day, I hated the Japanese for killing their son. I hated the Germans for killing the Jews in Europe. I felt frightened, threatened, and confused. War does that to everyone, and the violence and pain unleashed by fanatical and uncaring political leaders on innocent citizens remains, to my mind, unforgivable. In spite of all the patriotic war films we were shown back then, war had no attraction for me, and I came to hate it more than I hated the particular enemies of the United States, who so richly deserved enmity. Impressions formed in childhood are not easily changed. War and violence still fill me with loathing, even though in a world of terror I am convinced that pure pacifism is only a ticket to the early demise of and worthy societies. Yet I feel the prayer for peace which marks the conclusion of our daily *Amidah* prayer service should be given extra emphasis in our education and in our lives.

VE Day and VJ Day were special moments in my life. Everyone alive then felt that a terrible yoke had been removed from the shoulders of humanity. The world was going to have another chance after all, and we children felt that mankind would certainly take advantage of this new opportunity. We were then yet unaware of the true nature of our Soviet ally and of the other unpleasant realities of the world scene that would soon dawn upon us. Yet, 50 years later, I feel the world is in a better condition, even if only slightly better, than it was in the terrible first half of this century. The memories of the frightening past color my view of the tolerable present. I still hope for the bright future that I felt assured of as a young person 50 years ago. I hope that my children and grandchildren will live to see that better world unfold.